Another Book To Burn
The State of Scotland

Edited by J. N. Reilly

Bootleg *e*ditions

Dedication: To Big John for the paper: Freda Welch for her work on the typescript: Henry, John and Natasha for inspiration: Ann for more than I can say.

Acknowledgements: Thanks to Richard Demarco, Neil McNicol and Farquhar McLay for suggestions and encouragement, to Anne for giving me Louise Cockburn's number, and of course our printer, Tommy Kayes, and Joe Murray. Thanks also to Vernon Coleman for permission to publish *Requiem for the NHS* which first appeared in the Evening Times; John Taylor Caldwell for *Never Again* from his autobiography *Severely Dealt With,* published by Northern Herald Books, Bradford; the Scotia Review for John Manson's *Scotland-National and International.*
Myles Campbell's three poems from his collection *À Caradh an Rathaid,* published by Coisceum Dublin, appear for the first time in English translation in the present anthology.

Cover cartoon : Hugh Dodd
Cover design: J. N. Reilly

Bootleg editions 1998

ISBN: 0 9534280 0 1

Printed by Clydeside Press
37 High Street, Glasgow

Contents

Introduction *by J. N. Reilly*

Where there was hope there is now despair. The country has been betrayed by Tony Blair and New Labour. Instead of the much prayed for and expected reversal of Tory policies, the ideology of greed and contempt which has been laying waste to our communities, what do we get but more of the same: rising unemployment, and where there is employment, slave wages: a concerted attack on the most vulnerable and poorest people in our communities, including the disabled whose entitlement to state benefits is being eroded, not least by intimidation, a tactic also used against Poll Tax defaulters, the very people whose fight against Thatcherism helped Blair into office: and 16 and 17 year olds are still to be denied benefits. You can marry at 16, you can die for you're country at 16, but you're not worth benefits, you're not worth a decent minimum wage, you're not worth an education, which just about sums up what Blair and his acolytes think of you, no matter what age you are.

The NHS in decay, the education system in chaos, all our institutions to a greater or lesser extent suffering from financial and intellectual underinvestment and that poisonous mix of *sleaze* and *political correctness.* It's the same in the Scottish literary scene and with Scottish publishers; sadly a cottage industry compared to English publishing houses; where it's a matter of who you know rather than what you know – pucker up those lips and start kissing arse if you want a career – where if you don't like who they like and you don't hate who they hate, well, you know what to do.

There isn't a staff-room, office or board-room which isn't contaminated with the pernicious legacy of Thatcherism as now embraced and perpetuated by Blair and New Labour. And as if that isn't more than enough contamination to deal with, the very food we would like to afford to eat more of is under threat from the biotechnology corporations. Don't believe them when they say genetically modified food will feed the starving millions. Don't believe them when they say genetically modified food will be inexpensive. All they want is your money. Don't believe them when they say it's safe. They can't prove it's safe. And while corporations such as Monsanto, Zenecca and Novartis spread lies about the safety of genetically modified food, Blair is jumping from one politically correct hobby horse to another, such as the *drugs question,* allocating 217 million pounds for fighting the proliferation of drugs, when everyone but the ignorant and those with vested interests agree that no one should be criminalised for taking any drug and that through the legalisation of cannabis and other substances our economic and cultural well-being would be greatly enhanced.

What disgusting amounts of money Blair and New Labour are squandering! 200 million have also been allocated to *crime blackspots,* but not for education and jobs. Just like Thatcher Blair has no intention of attending to the root causes of crime, poverty, ill health and ignorance, because like Thatcher he believes in only the *free market.*

Added to the above, as you know, is the 750 million pounds being spent on the Millennium Dome, an inauspicious monument to New Labour's madness.

Forming around us is not the nanny state but the police state, controlled by the economics of multi-national corporations, in which you will have no choices.

Only the most fearful, ignorant or power hungry, would deny that it is now time for Scotland to take responsibility for itself, that it is now time to be responsible for ourselves, to grasp the potential of the new Scottish Parliament and move towards Independence in 2002, to take our place in the world and aspire to the finest human actions. The future is in your hands.

We are fortunate we can choose Independence, for think of our friends in the north of England and the Midlands, indeed throughout England, and even more so, all those nations such as Kashmir, Kosovo, Tibet and Palestine, each and every one desperate to lift the yoke of tyranny.

Wouldn't it be a fine and fitting gesture when our Parliament opens to return the Ghost Dance Shirt which is in the Kelvingrove Museum and Art Gallery, Glasgow, to the Lacota Sioux, by presenting it to Marcella Le Beau.

In the present anthology the joys, fears, hopes and desires of Scotland are given an eloquent voice by some of Scotland's finest poets, essayists, authors and artists.

It is now time to claim our Celtic/European cultural heritage, to create the Scotland we desire, to create the future.

In a place called Scotland, 23/24 Oct. 1998

Richie Venton

Slave Labour under New Labour

"We could build it in the Bahamas or Guyana where we are guaranteed 365 days a year good weather, but because of labour prices the choice is between Ireland and Scotland!"

So said Norman Nixon, brother of the late President of the USA, as he revealed plans to build a £6billion, mile-long ship intended as a floating tax haven for the obscenely rich. Fifty thousand of these bloated tax-dodgers would commute to shore by private yachts or aircraft. So the parasites are to exploit Scotland's pool of cheap Labour to facilitate tax-avoidance on their ill-gotten wealth. There is something rotten in the state of Scotland when it can slaughter the competition from Latin America in offering sweatshop labour to the globe's exploiters.

No wonder a huge clamour arose for a decent minimum wage over recent years, with over 85 per cent support in opinion polls. Even 75 per cent of Tory voters supported such a measure! This reflects a growing unease at not just the pitiful poverty suffered by millions, but also at the obscene and growing gulf of inequality in society. 447 billionaires own more wealth than half the world's population. In this country the gap between rich and poor is wider than at any time since records began in 1886.

Contrary to a common perception, those in poverty are not the unwaged alone. Certainly amongst the 14 million people living on the breadline are those cast onto the scrapheap of unemployment; those victimised for being sick or disabled; lone parents scapegoated and deprived of decent benefits; pensioners discarded like old dishcloths after a lifetime's contribution to society. But since the 1980s, those employed on low wages constitute the single biggest group in poverty in sweatshop Scotland. Of nearly two million workers in Scotland, 820,000 earn below two-thirds male median earnings, which is widely accepted as the low pay threshold. An incredible 452,000 Scots go to work for less than half male median earnings - £4.62 an hour in 1998 figures.

We met the security guard on £1.50 an hour. His company guard dog cost £3 an hour. It is widely believed that a dog is man's best friend, but that is plainly taking the piss. David Maclaine, boss of multi-million pound Edinburgh-based advertising agency McCann-Erickson pays himself £50,000 a year – which makes him a boardroom pauper! In mid-1998 he advertised for a chauffeur to be at his beck and call for 55 hours a week, for £50 a week, 90 pence an hour. The special bonus was free tea and coffee! And the qualities required for the job? Someone who is "reliable, honest, flexible, generally confident, happy, helpful and friendly." Not a mention of "insane"! As a bitter condemnation of wage levels in Scotland as we approach the New Millennium, and as a barometer of desperation and lowered expectations, 140 drivers applied for the job.

Lowered expectations are a serious barrier to human progress. Wage expectations have been systematically driven down over 20 years, as a vital part of driving down actual wages. Wages make up the lowest share of national wealth since records began in 1955; 62 % of Gross Domestic Producer in 1955, compared to 72% of GDP in 1975. Put more concretely, if wages as a proportion of the wealth produced by the working class had remained at 1975 levels, every worker would be over £50 a week better off. The whip of mass unemployment, casualisation, privatisation, part-time work, short-term contracts, youth 'training' schemes, abolition of benefits to 16-17 year olds, and the anti-union laws are amongst the arsenal deployed by the employers and Tories to achieve this wealth transfusion from poor to rich, from working class to capitalist class.

"You are lucky to have a job on any wage" is a tune that is set to reach a new crescendo as the looming recession bites.

A class of parasites thrives on other people's lowered expectations. Peter Mullen, Glasgow actor who won the 1998 Cannes Film Festival Best Actor Award, illustrated this anecdotally when he addressed the Scottish Socialist Alliance demo against slave labour in June 1998:

"Years ago my brother worked in Fairfield's shipyard as a cauker burner. He met a Norwegian girl and they moved to Oslo where he got himself a job as a labourer in a wee factory. Two days into the job and the shop steward comes up to him, tells him to put down his tools, that they're on strike. So he leaves along with the other workers and asks the shop steward what it's all about. The shop steward says: 'If we've told them once we've told them a thousand times, they either get that sauna fixed or we're out of here!' My brother told them that we too had confined rooms with slippery floors and steam rising – but we tended to call that the lavvy. It's all a question of self-worth."

Millions drowning in a sea of poverty saw New Labour's promise of a minimum wage as a potential lifeline, a rescue ashore to the firmer footing of a decent income. How disappointed, how betrayed, they now feel.

In 1992 Labour's election manifesto pledged an immediate "minimum wage of half male median earnings, rapidly rising to two-thirds male median earnings." In 1998 figures that would mean '£4.62 an hour, rapidly rising to over £6.'

In 1997, Blair's 'modernised', business-friendly New Labour studiously avoided raising such expectations, refusing to put a figure or formula forward, pledging instead to establish a Low Pay Commission after being elected to government.

This commission was the epitome of New Labour's oft-preached 'social partnership' with the employers. It was stuffed with fabulously paid academics, three token trade union leaders, and business representatives. The latter included the Human Resources Director for Granada, whose French companies have a more honest, explicit name: Exploitation de Meridien!

Granada pays barely subsistence wages to its workers in motorway service stations, Trust House hotels, Happy Eaters, bowling rinks, theme parks, night-clubs and TV shops. They recently took over Pall Mall cleaning contractors, who sacked the Hillingdon Hospital cleaners for rejecting a 20% pay cut. New Labour's selection of companies like Granada to sit on their Low Pay Commission was a crude case of appointing the brothel-keeper to investigate celibacy.

The Commission's role was to conduct an exercise in sham consultation, holding semi-secret meetings in Scotland's cities in obscure venues for an hour at a time, in the middle of the working day; not a recipe for mass workers' participation. Both their ears were turned to the dire warnings and special pleadings of wealthy big business, with a blind eye turned to the demands of the low paid.

The trade unionists on the Commission made trappist monks seem garrulous. They never uttered a word of dissent when the Commission recommended pathetically low figures for the minimum wage, and a list of exemptions that would make the worst dodgy insurance salesman blush.

Things have a habit of turning into their opposite. That is the fate of the minimum wage reform in the hands of New Labour. Their figures of £3.60 an hour for those aged over 22, and £3 for 18-21 year olds only institutionalise low pay, rather than eliminate it. Their exclusion of all workers under 18, trainees and apprentices of all ages, and the technically self-employed, is an exploiters' charter, without moral or economic justification.

Young workers are not exempt from eating or paying for their keep. 18-21 year olds cannot go into the supermarkets, sports-wear shops or rent offices and demand special youth prices.

The effect of New Labour's exemption clauses will be the replacement of older, slightly better-paid workers with lower-paid young staff, and the sudden blossoming of thousands of 'traineeships' to dodge paying a minimum wage. And the basement-level thresholds of £3 and £3.60 will be used to cut wages, not boost them. Already Glasgow-based Heatwise, part of the Wise Group which has been trumpeted by the New Labour government as the national model for their New Deal, has slashed their trainees' wages from £3.98 to £3.60 an hour, to match the minimum wage on offer. They are only the first known case of many to follow.

New Labour's proposals make mockery of the words 'national', 'minimum' AND 'wage'. It is time working-class people banded together to stop being ripped off by the employers and fobbed off by Blair's big business-dominated government. A decent level of national minimum wage for all over 16, trainees and apprentices included, is central to a struggle for justice, human dignity and a decent life that transcends mere existence.

We are frequently told of the virtues of Europe. But one notable omission from the Labour politicians' prattling on this subject is the European Decency Threshold. This is defined by the European Commission as:

"A decent standard of living taking account of the basic economic, social and cultural needs of workers and their families."

It is measured as 68% of average earnings. It says that in Scotland 1998, we need over £6 an hour – in fact £6.60 – to meet the bare necessities of a decent life. £240 for a 40 hour week is hardly asking for the moon and the stars. The average wage is currently £370 a week; £412 for males, £300 for female workers.

Contrary to the propaganda of the profiteers, industry could well afford it. Have you ever noticed those who warn us about pricing ourselves out of a job are always multi-millionaires, or politicians like Tony Blair on about £70 an hour? Presumably they have given themselves an 'exemption clause' from this argument. The executives of the top 100 companies have median earnings of £545,000; that's £270 an hour, not a week. The richest 25% of them are on well over £350 an hour. And that excludes perks, pensions and share options.

"It is our job to glory in inequality", declared the shameless Thatcher in 1991. And by her own obscene standards she was glorious, making Britain the second most unequal country in the world.

Seven years on, Peter 'Prince of Darkness' Mandelson tells us "Tony Blair shares Margaret Thatcher's rock-hard determination to deal with poverty"!?

The richest 1,000 parasites in Britain have increased their incomes by £10 billion in the year since Blair's election, an average of £5,000 an hour. Running at the front of this pack of wolves are home-grown Brian Souter and Ann Gloag of Stagecoach, Scotland's richest man and woman. Their personal wealth leapt by £60m in Blair's first year of office - £15,000 an hour each. Now we can grasp the meaning of Blair's New Britain.

£6 an hour minimum wage is entirely justified, and needed to escape the jaws of the poverty trap. A minimum wage set at lower levels can mean workers losing up to 96 pence in housing benefit, council tax rebates and Family Credit for every £1 gained in wages. And one of the formulae upon which £6 an hour is based – two-thirds male median earnings – is also a mechanism to combat the wage discrimination suffered by women workers, who make up 80% of the lowest paid. £6 an hour only seems a lot because the trade union leaders have helped Blair's New Tory government – and the Old Tories before them – to smash down people's expectations. Most trade union conferences, including the Scottish Trade Union Congress, adopted the formula of half male median earnings - £4.62 an hour minimum, without exemptions. This would increase the wages of 450,000 Scottish workers, although with lost benefits it would raise the actual incomes of much lesser numbers. But the trade union leaderships retreated from even this modest, inadequate compromise.

In submitting their claims to the Low Pay Commission, leaders of the TGWU and GMB backslided to calls for "not less than £4". For trade union bureaucrats on £70-80,000 plus chauffeured limousines and Gold Card accounts, the difference of 62 pence an hour appears irrelevant. For hard-pressed families it could put food on the table.

New Labour is fond of blood-curdling denunciations of the 'trade union barons' and of declarations of their independence of the unions. They have conducted a scorched earth policy on the rights and influence of ordinary trade unionists over government policy as New Labour retreats from any previous pretence of siding with the working class. But Blair also relies on the highly paid, often unelected bureaucracy of the trade unions to act as his Palace Guards, his bodyguards from the wrath of workers who expected change with the departure of the Tories. So the struggle for a decent minimum wage for all also necessitates a battle against the remote bureaucrats astride the unions, and for union democracy and socialist leaderships at every level, from the workplace upwards

The issue of a decent minimum wage lays bare the very nature of the beast known as free enterprise, the capitalist market economy. For many people struggling to cope with everyday life these may seem remote concepts. But the drive for maximised profits that is the very engine of capitalism, bears down on our daily lives like a modern Juggernaut, devouring all before it. The combined profits of big business in 1997 reached £131 billion. That is a staggering profit of well over £5,000 produced by every single worker, but going into the pockets of the billionaires and millionaires so beloved of Blair.

Imagine the benefits of public, social ownership of the giant transnationals, the big industries, banks, privatised utilities, construction companies and North Sea Oil; it's not so hard to picture. For a start, poverty could be banished, the terrible burden of worry and ill health which it feeds could be lifted, and profits for the parasites replaced by a life fit for humans, for millions of people.

We face a stark choice; continued slave labour under New Labour, or

14

a challenge to the profit-crazed system, based on the goal of a demo-
democratic socialist Scotland, pioneering an international battle for
socialism. It is time to lift our sights, lift our chins, and take up that
challenge, using the call for a decent minimum income as a sharp
weapon to champion the case for socialism in our lifetime.

Graham Fulton

The Rivers

The weans scoop manky stuff
from a stank with a stick,
giggle, ask the passers-by
'Do you believe in Jesus?'

Blow spiky hoots from blades of grass,
barefoot dance
in the clothespole gardens,
fearless among the King of the castle
dirty wee rascal piles of broken,
barking whippets, STOP
THE WARRANT SALE posters, tinsel
snagged on wire, jokers
ticking in bicycle spokes, a mush
of tissues smeared with red, a sofa
in the middle
                    of nowhere.

Someone sitting behind a desk
forgot to tell them
they don't exist.

Dee, Nith, Annan, Tweed.
Council streets named after water.
Future fossils. A teenage couple
bump their pram up blackweed steps

towards their curtains, the only splash
of life
in a block of boarded-up darkness.
Stairwells, landings, metal and mesh.
A headless doll the colour of flesh,
graffiti screams BEWARE THE BASTARD
DSS GRASSES FINDHORN MAFIA
CHIBMEN WILL GO DOWN
among the sniff dens,
cratered hieroglyph walls,
drug deal holes of smells and spray.

And hope
constructed with wheelie-bin crap.
Don, Forth, Lexwell, Tay.
Someone shouting 'Close that door!',
bedlam melodies, third-hand drumkits,
tinny guitars in cupboard bedrooms
thrash out over burnt
and fallen roofs, the orchards
of tangle and rage, brick battlefields
of a civil war,
                somewhere
a phone, connection, desire.

No-one told them they shouldn't ask,
no-one told them they have no chance
as they run to the Greensleeves
ice-cream van.
Gryffe, Orchy, Almond, Spey.
The rivers hug the side of the hill.

Someone at the back of a shadow
forgot to tell them
they've been ripped out,
forgot to tell them they've been

forgotten.

Snow White Down at the Whirlies

the punch-
bag woman

in her slippers

gets on
with things

hangs up
his favourite shirt to dry

snow white

where her blood-
stains were

Ritual Soup

Blood and mess
and sticky legs. and porridge
bubbling in the pot,
the hand sliding up the skirt,
the baby sliding down the canal
from nothing
to nothing, pass the parcel,
scissoring the umbilical. and it's okay

to do the Hokey Cokey, okay
to put your left leg out
in rain at the graveside,
mud on your shoes. and scrambling
for pennies among the confetti,

wedding bagpipes, wedding hats.
and queuing at subway ticket turnstiles,
coming home from work in the dark
from petrol pumps and shoeshop stools
and bitter beerhouse afternoons,
the drunken shivering making of love
in honeymoon hotels, funfair waltzers,
Palais smoocheramas. and it's okay

to do the dashing white sergeant.
breathing out, breathing in
the cold light of Auld Lang Syne,
feeling afraid that all there is
is blood and mess and sticky legs,
kisses and slaps and tasty drugs,
patterns of Hogmany puke in the close
at four in the morning, soup in the pot.
and corpses sliding down the canal,
scissors sliding up the skirt,
babies lowered into the hole from nothing
to nothing, musical chairs,
letting go of the cords. and it's okay

to shake it all about, it's okay
to do the Grand old Duke of York,
put pennies on your eyes. okay
to fertilise the dead,
join in the dance, pronounce yourself egg.

Sarah North

The Ultimate Threat to St. Kilda

St. Kilda lies in the Atlantic Frontier over a hundred miles west of the Scottish mainland. It is the most isolated and magical group of islands in the British Isles. Volcanic in origin, the islands have been gradually weathered into incredible, dramatic shapes. The sheer cliffs of St. Kilda rise majestically from the sea, wind-blasted and thrashed by waves. Its towering black cliffs and sea stacks surround grassy terraces, rugged valleys and bays. The starkness and beauty of St. Kilda – which is not one island but a group – is haunting. In 1947 the Naturalist James Fisher wrote: "Whatever he studies, the future observer of St. Kilda will be haunted the rest of his life by the place, and tantalised by the impossibility of describing it to those who have not seen it".

The St. Kilda archipelago is best known for its natural beauty both on land and in the surrounding seas, which are considered to be one of the most spectacular underwater landscapes in Britain. The crystal clear waters are famed for their marine life. Grey seals breed in the sheltered caves and coves and common seals are frequently seen from the islands. Below the waves lie rock arches, tunnels, caves and shelves swept by oceanic currents. They support expanses of beautiful jewel sea anemone, red sea-fingers and soft corals. The water is so clear that giant Kelp seaweed forests are found down to 150 metres, three times the normal depth.

The deep sea beyond, in the Atlantic Frontier, has been described as a "motorway" for migrating whales and dolphins, for which it is considered to be the richest habitat in Europe. Only last year the extremely rare and endangered Blue Whale was spotted, the first sighting of this species in two decades.

The St. Kilda archipelago is also one of the main sea-bird breeding areas of the North Atlantic. There are approximately 400,000 breeding pairs of 15 species of sea bird. St. Kilda is the breeding site of the largest assembly of gannets in the world.

St. Kilda's natural beauty is complimented by its fascinating history. For over 2000 years these isolated lands were home to a community of people who survived in St. Kilda's harsh environment by living communally; sharing their food, tools and land and conserving their precious resources through sustainable farming activities. It was not until the 18th century when contact with the mainland increased that this population became impacted by visitors such as religious missionaries and tourists who incidentally brought in their wake influences from mainstream society like disease and money. By the beginning of this century the St. Kildans' traditional culture had become eroded and a mixture of hunger, disease and out-migration diminished the population. On the 29th August 1930 the remaining 36 St. Kildans were finally evacuated from the islands.

St. Kilda is so special that in 1986 it was designated a World Heritage site, putting its natural magnificence alongside internationally recognised locations like the Great Barrier Reef and the Grand Canyon. The aim of World Heritage Site designation is the "protection of natural and cultural sites of global significance, based on criteria of universal value and integrity" and the UK Government is responsible to "ensure identification, protection, conservation, presentation and transmission to future generations of the cultural heritage on its territory".

But today the islands of St. Kilda, and the ocean surrounding it, are under threat. Incredibly, the UK Government wants to develop the beautiful Atlantic Frontier for oil. In 1997 alone they offered over 22,000 square miles to 30 multi-national oil companies. This development threatens the natural environment of St. Kilda through both the risk of a major oil spill incident and the inevitable, continuous background pollution that will be derived from the activities of the oil industry..

Some oil fields in the Atlantic Frontier have already been developed to produce oil. Enormous floating vessels are being used to pump oil from the seabed because the ocean is too fierce and deep for ordinary oil rigs. Shuttle tankers and supply ships scuttle to and from land to transport oil and supplies. The first field that has produced oil in this area is called Foinaven and is run by BP. Within 13 days a technical failure caused an oil spill.

Many more areas of the Atlantic Frontier are destined to become developed in the future. The UK Government is already planning to offer yet more plots of seabed on the Atlantic Frontier for oil exploration in the years 1999, 2000, 2001. The Atlantic Frontier looks doomed to become a massive marine industrial estate.

The oil industry is trying to conquer the Atlantic Frontier, fighting the wind and waves to get to its prize. There are two great ironies to this tragedy. The first is that they are searching for a resource that the world can no longer afford to use. Work by international scientists shows that we can only afford to burn a quarter of the world's known oil reserves before causing dangerous and irreversible effects from climate change. The second is that the very elements that act as an obstacle to the oil industry's work are the clean source of our future energy needs; wave, wind and solar.

Greenpeace believes that new oil production in areas like the Atlantic Frontier is totally unjustifiable. More oil will not only cause damage to the local environment and places like St. Kilda but, when burned, also threatens the climate. We are campaigning for political action to be taken to stop new oil production and bring in clean, sane energy alternatives. We are also calling on the United Nations to protect the World Heritage Site of St. Kilda from this oil development.

Last year the captain of the MV Greenpeace sent the following message from the Atlantic Frontier: "It is clear to me why I should be here. Humans want to turn the wilderness into a wasteland; to desecrate all that is pristine, free, wild and clean – to blemish and sully; to take it upon ourselves to intrude beyond our right. The Tao Teaching says "when men lack a sense of awe, there will be a disaster."

It is said that St. Kilda's genius loci or "spirit of place" casts a spell on all who go there. Most of us will never visit St. Kilda but the bewitching spirit of these islands, their history, solitude and splendour, is our children's heritage.

For centuries St. Kilda was insulated from the outside world "safe in its own whirlwinds and cradled in its own tempests" (Dr Macculloch 1819) but as this wall of isolation began to crumble so too did the sustainability of its community. Now its very land and seas lie in the pathway of unsustainable modern development.

Myles Campbell

Loss and Gain

They came, first, and deprived us
of our freedom,
the freedom to fight to protect.
Things were moving, improving,
better cannon and new ways of killing,
the tacksmen exiled
and the chiefs with the love of gold.
But the mountains remained
and the deer were still on Creag Uanach.

They came and took away
our life and living from the land,
the best soil for rocks and turf.
But still we kept the tie between us and earth,
scraping a living from sheaf and gleaning,
milk from the cow, and when necessary,
a trout from the stream.

They came and gave us
a new education with new equipment.
There was no need any more for crofts,
for cattle or the planting
of seed in the ground.
But the mountains remained.

They deprived us of the ancient knowledge,
the old tales of the old ways,
our heritage, and in their place they put
new songs to make a new heart.

They gave us cars, supermarkets,

Maoilios Caimbeul

Bhuainn agus Dhuinn

Thàinig iad agus thug iad bhuainn
ar saorsa an toiseach,
an t-saorsa sabaid gus dìon.
Bha cùisean a' gluasad, a' dol am feabhas,
canan na b' fheàrr agus dòighean ùra air marbhadh,
na fir-bhaile air am fuadach
agus na cinn-fheadhna le gaol an òir.
Ach mhair na beanntan
agus bha na fèidh fhathast air Greag Uanach.

Thàinig iad is thug iad bhuainn
comas tighinn beò air an tìr,
am fearann a b' fheàrr airson creagan is riasg.
Ach fhathast chum sinn an ceangal eadarainn 's an talamh,
sinn beò air èiginn air sguab is dlòth,
bainne na bà agus, nuair a dh'fheumte,
breac as an allt.

Thàinig iad is thug iad dhuinn
foghlam ur is innealan ùra.
Cha robh feum tuilleadh air craitean,
air crodh no air sìol
a chur anns an talamh.
Ach mhair na beanntan.

Thug iad bhuainn an seann eòlas,
na sgeòil air an t-seann dòigh,
ar dualchas, agus nan àite chuir iad
òrain ùra bha dèanamh a' chridhe às ùr.

Thug iad dhuinn càraichean, supermarkets,

gear without end, development boards,
fish farms, shellfish farms,
deer farms, nuclear power,
electric light, water on tap,
visitors and people who stay,
people who stay and people who frequent.
They came and gave us.
But the mountains will remain.

They gave us money,
all the city's mod cons,
sin and grace,
rubbish and polluted water.
Great wide roads through the glens.

They found what they sought –
nature enslaved and power
over life and death.
A finger on the button.
Like a god.
Isn't it wonderful how well you have done?
But the mountains will remain.

The Stone

I grip the purity stone
from circumstance to circumstance,
wave-moving, tide-heaving,
amidst the small and great stones,
I grip it with a deathly grip.
And always the sea
shifting, polishing it, making us
closer together, splitting us.
I can't think
of a time when you weren't there.
But also, at the same time,
I sometimes think you are just a dream.

innleachdan gun chrìch, bùird leasachaidh,
ionadan àrach èisg, ionadan àrach maoraich,
tuathanachas fhiadh, cumhachd niùclasach,
solas an dealain, uisge sa ghoc,
luchd-turais agus luchd-fuirich,
luchd-fuirich agus luchd-tathaich.
Thàinig iad is thug iad dhuinn.
Ach mairidh na beanntan.

Thug iad dhuinn airgead,
uile ghoireasan a' bhaile,
peacadh agus gràs,
sgudal agus uisgeachan truailte.
Rathaidean mòra farsaing tro na glinn.

Fhuair iad na bha iad a' lorg –
nàdur fo cheannsail agus cumhachd
beatha is bàis.
Corrag air a' phutan.
Mar dhia.
Nach eil e mìorbhaileach cho math 's a rinn sibh?
Ach mairidh na beanntan.

A' Chlach

Tha clach na gileid na mo dhòrn
a' dol o chùis gu cùis,
mùthadh thuiltean, luaisgean chuantan,
am measg nan clachan beag is mòr,
is greim a' bhàis agam oirre.
Agus an còmhnaidh a' mhuir
ga gluasad, ga lìomhadh, gar dlùthadh
ri chèile, gar sgaradh.
Chan urrainn dhomh smaoineachadh
air àm anns nach robh thu ann, a chlach.
Ach cuideachd aig an aon àm
bidh mi a' smaioneachadh nach eil annad ach aisling.

Irina Ratushinskaya

Isn't it strange how small the world is,
yourself under the bear's paw,
crying that things aren't quite right
in the great country where everyone is a brother.
We under the bull's arse
and the smell not very becoming;
mouse-squeaking in our own archipelago,
moaning for our Odessa and the roots
engulfed by the sea.
But, o God, in the heat and frost
of your cell,
at least you will not feel shame
for the things you haven't done
or for the love you gave to the spirit.

Irina Ratushinskaya

Nach neònach cho beag 's a tha an saoghal,
thusa fo spàg a' mhathain,
a' sgiamhail nach eil cùisean buileach ceart
anns an duthaich mhòir
far a bheil a h-uile duine na bhràthair.
Sinne fo thòin an tairbh
's gun am fàileadh ro chùbhraidh;
a' luch-bhìgeil nar n-archipelago fhìn,
a' caoidh ar n-Odessa 's na reumhan
air na shiab a' mhuir.
Ach, a Dhè, ann an grìos agus reothadh
do chealla,
cha bhi nàire ortsa co-dhiù
airson na nithean nach do rinn thu
no airson a' ghràidh a thug thu dhan spiorad.

Bill Robertson

Spinning the Punter Along

When it comes to burying its citizens under piles of political bullshit, then Glasgow's certainly Miles Better. Around £1 million a year is spent by the city council – on its team of spin doctors.

Tony Blair may claim that "open government" is one of New Labour's priorities. But, down at street level, the punters complain of being kept, like mushrooms, in the dark.

There are times, at George Square, when even cynical observers, like me, feel the mind drifting off to some municipal Brigadoon. In my case, to the old burgh of Kinghorn.

It received its royal charter in the 13th century and up until the re-organisation of local government in the 1970s, it still had its own town council. In fact, Kinghorn at the time of its demise had the distinction of being Scotland's smallest.

There was a provost, eight councillors and less than 2000 houses. The council's way of doing business probably had changed very little over the centuries. It was based on truly open government.

Everything was in public. Even the bank books, I recall, were on the table. Just in case someone had run off with the money. Tenders for a contract? All the bids were read out. Interviews for a typist's job? The mothers were there in the public gallery making sure that each applicant had a fair hearing.

The ratepayers paid the bills and expected to see how every pound was spent. Passing along the street, a wee woman would remind the scaffie "Ye'er no paid to lean of yer shovel".

Scotland's municipal structure has changed yet again. Not necessarily for the better. Finance has become so complicated that few councillors pretend to fully understand it. And even fewer taxpayers.

The traditional town clerk has vanished. Yesterday's big men have been replaced by a new breed of obedient servants. Today's young officers, seeking promotion, quickly learn to go with the flow.

This new breed of executive is, shall we say, amenable. Even pliable. Their first allegiance tends to be to their political masters, rather than to their profession. After all, when it comes to appointments, councillors allot the top jobs.

Which explains why it is so easy, in today's world, for the politicians to control the system. To restrict the information flow. To determine just what the public should be allowed to know. Officials, all too often, play along with the game.

Meanwhile, whatever happened to the long promised Freedom of Information Act? There is no sign of it on the parliamentary agenda for 1999.

Alex Cathcart

Praetorian Guard of Caesar Brown's New Deal Reserve Army

Only one little bugger to listen to, and if he had been here last week like the rest of them the bloody Register could be filled in and finished with. Still, could be worse, quite often some of these fuckers keep you waiting right up to the last day before the holidays. Ach, one's not too bad. Not too bad at all. Give him the floor and Pass him and be done with him and Bob's your Uncle. Hang on behind, do the Regi and whacko! that's another step nearer the door. Ah ya beauty. Wonder if she's got the flight tickets yet? Been better driving. Still. Bit of the luxury at holiday time is quite in order. Everybody does it. Or should anyway. Need to bring back a wee bit more wine this year. That was good stuff.

And he's here. Good. "How y'doin, Michael? Missed you last week. Everything O.K?"

"Awright."

"Good. See the game last night?"

"Seen the second half."

"You never missed much. The first was execrable. Really dire. I'm glad I never went. A friend of mine offered me his season ticket for the Stand, full Hospitality, too, the lot, y'know up beside the Directors' Box? But, ach I really didn't think it was going to be a good game. I think I was right, eh? Mind you it's always good to see that Italian bloke play. He's some player isn't he?"

"Aye. He's Yugoslav."

"Is he? There you go. His name sounds Italian too. I don't think they'll hold on to him for next season do you?"

"Dunno."

"I don't think so.

Right. Let's do the Register.   Michael Robert Andrews"

"Hu."

"Sorry?"

"Here."

"Thank you. Well. the rest get their Mark because they finished last week. But never mind you've only got this one Assessment then you can be off. I'll have to stay here and finish off this Register, but you can go. And that'll be you and I finished. Unless I see you next Session for some class or other. Are you coming back to do something else? What is it you're doing just now?"

"Fabrication and Welding Introductory."

"Well that's good. Is that John Squire's course?"

"Aye."

"Good bloke John isn't he?"

"Aye, he's awright."

"Just all right, eh?"

"Aye."

"So what would you do if you came back next year? Fabrication and Welding Two?"

"They're no runnin a course."

"Oh. How's that?"

"Never get enough people."

"That right?"

"Aye"

"When you think how the country needs tradesmen too. Did you know there are firms that can't get the skilled tradespeople they need?

29

I blame that last lot. And the Unions. For years they've let the old apprenticeships be whittled away. Now they're reaping the whirlwind. There are just not enough skilled people around."

"So how's Mr. Squires no runnin a course then?"

"Oh, I'm sure John wants to run a course. John's a good bloke. It's all this business with funding. If we don't get enough bums on seat in a class then we cant run the course and that means keen young men like yourself lose out."

"There's only four in the class."

"I know, it's just that you're from the, you and the rest of the lads are, it's just the way it's funded, you guys get funded. Well, I'm sorry to hear, eh, John's course isn't running. That's a shame. So, where were we?"

"Dunno."

"Register. Yes, that's you up-to-date. You've attended well. Well done.

"Yes. You've attended well. The Assessment. Might as well get it done, eh?"

"Might as well."

"Right. This is Assessment Four. Oral Presentation. Basically, you've just got to talk about something for three minutes, answer a few Questions about it, and then, Bob's your Uncle. Is that all right? Any subject. Anything at all. just keep it reasonably Structured, remember: beginning, middle and end; introduction, body of the work and conclude. So, a bit of locution and that's it."

"Aye. Right."

"So. O.K. then? But remember what the man said: Perspicuity and brevity are not necessarily two horses that can be harnessed together."

"Aye. Perspex and bevy."

"Eh? Oh. Aye, right, good. I'll need to remember that one, Mick."

"Michael."

"Oh sorry. I keep forgetting. Michael. I keep getting you confused with   "

"That's O.K."

"Right. What's it to be then, Michael? What's your talk to be about?"

"Well I never knew what to talk about, politics n that or whatever, so I just thought I'd tell you about my weekend."

"Your week-end? That's good, it's good, eh, but, ah, a whole week-end, poo, that's maybe making a bit hard for yourself. In terms of the time, I mean. I think your week-end would take more than the three minutes to tell about. Why don't you just make it, say, the Saturday. Or the Sunday even."

"Never get up to much on a Sunday. Place is a mortuary where I live."

"Och, I know. I know. That's the Scottish Presbyterian legacy. It's getting better though. at least we can get a pint on a Sunday now and get the kids away to the parks. I remember when even the parks were shut on a Sunday. I mean, a Park for goodness sake. Now we even get the football on a Sunday so it is getting better.

And the supermarkets are open as well aren't they? Although I think it's funny a person can't buy a carry-out on a Sunday until after twelve. I mean, hey, what about people that don't go to church? And what if you get people over suddenly and you decide to have a wee barbie?

So Michael. What do you reckon? Just make it the Saturday?"

"In my bed on Sunday anyhow."

"Right. Good. O.K., whenever you're ready just go out to the front there and you can start anytime."

"There?"

"Sure. Just stand at the desk, it's only a desk. Don't lean back on it mind, be confident, stand up on your legs, just relax and speak. You can pretend to be the teacher teaching me something."

"I'll just talk about my Saturday."

"Right. Just wait a sec, till I get this Check-list started. I've passed your Dress and stuff don't worry about that, I mean this is only Communications Two. Right then, Michael, whenever you're ready. Ope. I'll just take my watch off and place it here, time you."

"Well Ma came in and got me out the bed. Just timmed me out on the sheets. I never bothered wi a shower. I don't think I took a breakfast, aye, I did. I had a bowl o Crunchies. It was time for Gary Lineker, so I just watched that. Ma gave me another cup o tea. Lineker was his usual rubbish, but that Liverpool guy was quite funny. I like him. He tells the truth. He tells you what's going on when the they're making the moves. He's good at using that white sort of chalk line on the computer and telling you what they were thinkin when they were daein whit they were daein. He's a good teacher.

When it finished I got ready and went up the street. there was a couple o guys there wi a baw so we had a wee kickabout but I got fed up and went off tae ma pal James's.

He's got the Nintendo and that stuff.

He's really crackin at it. He had a new game: Target Choice. At first I was diabolical but after a wee bit it was better. It's a good game if you ever see it, but ye must pick the right target to attack or you've had it.

Ye jist get sucked further and further intae this Lagoon that's pure poison sort of quicksand stuff. It's good.

We went out about tea-time. Jamesy wanted to score but I talked him out of it, we had nae cash anyhow and drummin's useless in the summer unles we get somebody havein a barbie and maybe all at the back o the place. Met Chico. I think he had you as a teacher as well. He says he thinks he knows ye anyhow. He's pretty sure he thinks he knows ye. Chico was off for some videos for his Da and was getting tae pick a movie for himself, so we tagged on wi him and walked tae the rental place. Chico likes that horror stuff, it's not bad but. We went back to Chico's and watched the vidoes.

His Da's stuff was crap, but he gave us a couple o beers each so we never said too much, at least never tae his face. They were O.K I suppose. The special effects were no bad.

Chico's Da went off for a kip and left us to it. The video was shite, sorry. Sorry. It was useless. Anyhow. Em. That was it.

Jamesy and me went up the street, but there was not a soul anywhere. It was really dead, for a Saturday.

We just stood at the close and blethered. Two polis were comin so we just called it a day.

Ma and Da were watchin the late movie, so I went up to the room and played some records.

That's it.   I think. I just went to bed then.

That's it.

Saturday."

"Good, Michael. That was good. That was quite interesting. In terms of Structure you just used the chronology of your day: from rising to going back to bed. Good.

There were a few colloquialisms here and there 'crap' for instance, I mean that's almost as bad as the sshh word. but that's O.K. don't worry about that, I forget myself sometimes. Your Pace was good. Yeh, your Pace was just about right. Good.

I liked the 'timmin oot' the bed; it reminded me of when my mother used to do that to me, only it was to make the bed ready for my old man coming in from the night shift. Ach. Those were the days. Right. So what's left: Diction, O.K., Tone, O.K., ach, you don't have to worry about Grammar so much here Michael this is only Communication Two."

"How was my Perspex and Bevy?"

"Eh? Oh. Aye. Fine. Ha. Ha Aha. Not bad at all, my son. Now. Let's see. Body Language, no bother, Style, a bit Terse now and again, but O.K.. really, you know, Michael I would say your style is Vigorous. Vigorous."

"Does that mean I've passed then?"

"Passed? Aye, of course, this is me you are talking too. We'll skip the Question and Answer session, eh? I mean if you don't know what your Saturday was all about, who does?"

"Right. I'm off then."

"Aye sure, away ye go, man, an see your mates. Go to it, young man. Enjoy your summer. Maybe see you next year?"

"Maybe. I'll talk tae somebody. See ye."

"See ya."

Woof. Register. Four crosses. Michael Andrews: Communications Two. All passed, and no problems. Not a bad wee lad that, really. All things considered. Bit angry though. It was there in his Body Language. Hope he picks the right target, or he'll get sucked down into that muddy Lagoon he was talking about. Metaphorically speaking. Need to watch at the next barbie though.

William Hershaw

Exorcising Mary King's Close

My grandfather, who was a coal miner in Lanarkshire and Fife, once told me, "At least you know where you stand with a Tory, son. He's your natural enemy and he'll not try to hide it. Him and his family will have been highly successful at hanging on to their advantages over the years and they'll fight like hell to keep it that way."

He once told me that he had attended a meeting in the small village of Forth where the speaker was Alec Douglas Home, at that point a prospective parliamentary candidate on the vote trail. An erudite miner in the audience, educated under the auspices of the trade unions, decided to wind the then young, would-be politician up a bit. In his thickest yokel voice he claimed to have read a proposal that the Highlands of Scotland could be regenerated by establishing banana plantations - was this a feasible option? The reply was delivered in the most patronising of tones by the stuttering patrician politician, "A capital idea, my good man, and one I will surely look into when I am returned as your Member of Parliament."

It sounds like a yarn out of John Buchan but, apocryphal or not, it reveals my grandfather's sound grasp of the nature of politicians and politics. He could remember the establishing of the ILP and he could reel off a long list of Scottish leftist fire-brands who had turned into tame establishment figures, emasculated by seats in Westminster, careers, honours, titles and other geegaws of the British Crown. To him, Lord Shinwell was a contradiction in terms. God knows what he would have thought of Tony Blair (Tommy Bear, as my son calls him) and New Labour – the NLP.

As a child growing up in the sixties I cannot recall my mum and dad discussing politics. I would be very surprised if they were not voting Labour during this period. It was a time of relative increasing affluence for us. By that I mean that at the start of the decade a bottle of Irn Bru was a luxury that had to be budgeted for and by 1970 we could go for a run in the car on a Sunday and stop off for a High Fish Tea on the road home. For some reason, during this time, I made up my mind that I was going to join the Scottish National Party as soon as I was sixteen. I'm not really sure to this day why this was so – it certainly wasn't due to any powerful economic argument as there are few twelve year old boys who are susceptible to these. It may have had something to do with Winnie Ewing's victory in nearby Hamilton in 1967 or Scotland's marvellous Wembley win in that annus mirablis. I can remember getting a book out of Motherwell library that told of how the Sioux and the Cheyenne had their land stolen by the Pale faces. A few weeks later I read an account of the massacre of Glencoe. I think, even at that precocious age, I was able to make a connection. It was not easy to find the true history and identity of Scotland and I can understand now why it was and is kept so well hidden. I kept my vow and signed on as soon as I could.

Now, I am not a joining or a team person and I was bitterly disappointed by the diet of endless arguments about jumble sales in stale, empty, freezing halls. At first, I felt I had nothing in common with the rank and file of the Gordon Wilson led seventies S.N.P. Where was the romantic struggle, so nobly advocated by John MacLean and MacDairmid? My grandfather could never figure the S.N.P. out. He placed them, wrongly, alongside the liberals, a lily-livered bunch he despised because they were surrogate Tories with spray-on consciences. My nadir as a party activist came when I was chased by a crop-headed sailor wearing only union jack underpants while canvassing in the Rosyth Dockyard area.

And what of the rank and file of the S.N.P. back then? Looking back, I can see now that apart from wanting independence for Scotland they tended to be independently-minded types, often from better-off working class backgrounds. They rejected the reservation handout mentality in favour of standing up for themselves. In the main they were practical, good-hearted folk with a sense of social justice that began at home. I met with few instances of anti-English racism, the general perception being that the Scots only had themselves to blame for their predicament and that they could extricate themselves from it if they had the gumption and the vision. There were a lot of pragmatic people (contrary to the portrayed image) who had the nouce to see that the Labour Party were conning the Scottish people by claiming to represent them while denying them any legislative power. They were not the sorts to rat out and run abroad – there was a great love of the land itself among them. I was often disappointed by the comparative lack of interest in language and history – these were not folk who were looking backwards but ahead. They were also looking sideways at Eire, Denmark, Norway, etc. The main negative vibe was always directed, sometimes unfairly, at the Labour Party and even back then there was a deep distrust of Labour sleaze, carve-ups and jobs for the boys.

As with any political organisation there were a number of people involved for the wrong reasons and out to make a career for themselves. There was also a fringe of betartanned loonies who liked to march about in colour parties and recreate the glamour days of Bonnie Charlie. Embarrassing though they were, these nationalistic drag queens were harmless enough. In the cold light of dawn, their claymores subsided, they turned out to be small businessmen who were half - English.

Now it is almost commonplace to write about Labour corruption but back then to be "Nat", as the Daily Record dubbed you, was to invite much ridicule and open hostility. The up and coming Brian Wilsons and Helen Liddells regarded you, ideologically, as Ian Paisley regards Gerry Adams. On a good day you were a naïve idiot trying to turn the clock back but mostly, pre-Salmon, you were a "Tartan Tory", a betrayer of the solidarity of the Scottish working class. This was an epithet which wounded me deeply.

Then, one day, Mr Dewar changed all that. These are difficult times for folk like me and I suspect they are going to get worse. In the long term I might end up taking out English citizenship. You see, going back to my grandfaither, I knew it all along. If a politician, economist or financier tells you that something won't work, it stands to reason that he has a vested interest in saying that. There is more than a good chance that a) he's lying, or b) he doesn't know. Most things will work if there is a will to make it so. And the wealthy sorts who would leave Scotland if it ever became independent? Not if there's a buck in it for them. The galling thing for me is that all those opinionated clowns who stalled, blocked and prevaricated, telling me "it wouldn't work" for years while the oil dried up are now painting their big faces/arses blue and white and yelling "Freeeeeeedom!" from the rooftops. Thanks to the hauf-wey hoose it is now possible for all sorts of unionists time-servers and honours acceptors to fudge the issue, trendily wearing their bravehearts on their sleeves while pushing in the queue for seats in the Assembly (a split infinitive and mixed metaphor sums up my rage).

You see, I'm just jealous because my private dream, my personal Scotland, is going to be spoiled by the takers, the talkers and the chancers. And there's one final thing. I have no quibble with anyone who wishes to call themselves British, North British, Northumbrian, Citizen of the World, whatever. But why should you be allowed to call yourself Scottish if you don't recognise and support the right of the Scottish people to govern themselves independently, sovereignly and separately? Why would you want to in the first place unless you were practising some form of deceit? Wearing a football jersey and greetin at the New Year doesn't make you Scottish – it makes you a cartoon. Just be honest.

And so on to Mary King's Close: an Edinburgh street blocked off by the authorities and the people left to die from the plague. Said to be haunted. The pomposity of the City Chambers now built over it. Recently it was decided to charge tourists for excursions down it. A perfect image for a poem.

Mary King's Close

First, to find the Founders
and set the plague ghosts free
we ripped down the two hypocrite flags,
ransacked the City Chambers
but found no one,
not even a tourist party.

They had dug theirsels in, gone down deep.
We flattened above ground with bulldozers,
then began to excavate.

As we worked doon, layer on layer,
we met up wi nae resistance
but uncovered groups
who had committed sideways;
receptions of unionist politicians and fixers,
arts council and tourist boards,
meetings of non-teaching educationalists,
pantomimes of show business celebrities,
admirers of royalty, non-reviewers of poetry,
fawners and fillers of honours lists.

In the very bottom passage we caught
Lulu, Brian Wilson and Ally McCoist
burning books by Henrysoun and Dunbar,
Donald Dewar was pouring petrol ower the bones
of the last wolf o Caledon.

And, at last, it was done.

They had hidden awthing doon thonder
that they couldnae thole,
stuffed a culture doon a hole,
and mair asides:
We brocht up hunners o skeletons;
whures fae Leith,
addicts fae Craigmillar,
ex-miners fae Danderha',
singel mithers and broukit bairns,
beggars, buggers and hale Aids hospices,
methmen and misfits, a' buried lang ago,
below the City offices.
Then we sat aroond the rim and wept for the plague ghaists.
Then we did our dance and in a dream
Crazy Horse and Joe Corrie said tae us,

"Let the licht fa in here!
Let the caller air blaw this killin clarty stoor awa!
We build anew,
and our parliament hoose will stand here.
Ower this hole we will heeze a teppee,
The bow o the stars will be its roof tree,
its daeins for a' the world tae see."

Les Ward

Removing Something Unpleasant From our Way of Life

The case against hunting with dogs is simple. It is that in a civilised society to chase and kill wild animals merely for pleasure is unnecessary, cruel and should be abolished and that if control should ever become necessary, it should be undertaken as quickly and efficiently and humanely as possible.

To the majority of the public and Members of Parliament these statements are not only reasonable but right. But to those who inflict this cruelty, suffering and death, the minority, they are statements to be played down as much as possible. This is not surprising when you consider what their so-called sporting pleasures actually involve.

Several weeks prior to the start of the main fox-hunting season, which runs from November until April, the young and inexperienced hounds are taken with older hounds to be initiated into the chasing and killing of foxes. This is referred to as "blooding" them. Their quarry is the fox-cubs born in the spring and now approximately six months old. Aware of the location of a fox – say in a wood – the hunt surrounds it with horses and riders. The hounds are then taken into the wood to chase and kill the cubs. The cubs stand no chance. They are, literally, driven into the mouths of the hounds and torn up piecemeal.

After weeks of training the hounds are ready for the start of the hunting season at the beginning of November. The hunt moves to a pre-selected location where, during the early hours of the morning, an "earth-stopper" has been out to block up the entrances of known fox earth's. When the animal returns after spending the night searching for food it is denied refuge underground and is forced to lie above ground. The hounds are sent in to flush out the fox. During the early stages of the chase, the fox easily outpaces the hounds. The terrified animal attempts to lose the pack but the fox, not being a natural prey species, is not physically evolved for a prolonged pursuit. After about an hour it is either caught and savaged by the pack of hounds or, perhaps, goes to ground in an unblocked earth. However, even underground, the fox is not safe because at this point the terrier-men who follow the hunt are called in. These individuals put their dogs down the earth in an attempt to "bolt" the fox and force it to run for its life again or they dig down to where the fox is under attack from the terrier and, once exposed, the fox is shot.

Like foxes, deer suffer a similar fate. At the start of the chase, 10-15 of the most experienced hounds are used to send the stag running. After about an hour of the chase, the remaining hounds in the pack are introduced. With the stag still fresh it rapidly outpaces the hounds with the speed and grace which is the hallmark of its species. However, as the afternoon wears on and tiredness begins to take its toll, the stag looks for other means of shaking off the hounds. He may run back to the security of his herd or seek sanctuary in thick gorse bushes where the hounds are unwilling to follow, but the riders and foot-followers quickly chase him out. After several hours, the superior stamina of the hounds begins to tell and they close in on the exhausted animal. The stag often seeks a final sanctuary in a river. Standing in mid-stream, he can defend himself with his antlers from the baying hounds. However, when the riders and followers catch up, the stag is killed with a shotgun or pistol.

Sometimes the hounds catch the deer in an open field, in woodland, or entangled in barbed wire. When this happens the hunt supporters rush in and wrestle the deer to the ground, holding it there until such time as it can be shot. The "kill" only occurs after a prolonged and exhausting chase. As with foxes, parts of the hunted animal's carcass are then removed and shared amongst the supporters. (Hunting deer with hounds is illegal in Scotland.)

Mink hunting is a summer blood sport and is the replacement for otter hunting. Otters were literally hounded to the brink of extinction by hunting. The hounds are followed on foot as they meander up and down the river banks and swim from side to side. When mink are scented there is a short chase before the exhausted victim seeks sanctuary, perhaps in a hole in the bank, in a drain or up a tree. They may be dug out and killed or 'bolted' and hunted again.

Hares are also hunted. Packs of three different breeds of hounds are used – beagles, bassets and harriers. As with all hunting with packs of dogs the victim is beaten, not by speed, but by stamina. Its speed gives the hare the early advantage – however the hounds' superior stamina wears down the hare to exhaustion. When first hunted and fresh, hares run in large circles, reluctant to leave their home range but, as they tire, they are overwhelmed by the dogs and killed.

Hares are also coursed by two dogs (usually greyhounds) which compete with each other in pursuit of their quarry. The hares are driven over a distance of half a mile or more into the coursing field. The two dogs, straining at the leash, are released and the already tired hare then has to run for its life. When both dogs catch the quarry, the hare can become a living rope in a tug-of-war being pulled and torn between the two dogs. The screaming hare's agony may last several minutes, depending on how quickly the handlers reach the dogs.

For decades the animal welfare movement has campaigned to bring an end to the barbaric blood sport of hunting with dogs. Recent years have seen growing optimism that this goal was getting ever closer and reached an all-time high in June 1997 when Labour MP, Michael Foster, was drawn first in the Private Member's Bill ballot and introduced his *Wild Mammals* (*Hunting with Dogs*) *Bill* into Parliament.

The aim of the Bill was to enhance the protection of wild animals from cruelty by outlawing 'sports' that involved hunting with dogs. It did not affect any other 'sport' such as fishing and shooting, or the right of landowners and tenant farmers to use dogs to control rabbits and rodents on their land, and did not affect an innocent dog walker whose dog suddenly takes off after a wild mammal.

Faced with ever-increasing opposition to hunting with hounds, pro-bloodsports groups under the banner of the Countryside Alliance organised a rally in London's Hyde Park in July 1997 in defence of their 'sports' and to oppose the Bill. There is surely something distasteful about taking part in a rally lobbying for the continuation of a pastime which is solely dedicated to the sadistic and cruel custom of tormenting and killing wild animals merely for pleasure.

The rally failed to change the views of MPs who, when the Bill came before the house for its Second Reading in November 1997, gave it a massive endorsement with 411 MPs voting in favour of the Bill and 151 against. Having successfully passed its Second Reading, the Bill entered its committee Stage and returned to the House in March 1998 to begin its Report Stage, the time when a Private Member's Bill is at its most vulnerable because of the limited time available for debate.

Pro-hunt MPs had made it known that they intended to submit amendments at this stage and if any of the amendments were not fully debated – and these MPs planned it to be the case – then the Speaker would be obliged to rule that the Bill had not been fully considered and it would fall. The pro-hunt MPs, true to their word, tabled hundreds of amendments, derailing the Bill and leaving its chances of becoming law as nil. In July 1998, with the Government refusing to give any of its time to ensure the Bill's success, Michael Foster was left with little choice but to withdraw his Bill. This was done in order to avoid his opponents from prolonging the debate which in turn would have blocked other back-bench legislation.

It is a sad day for democracy and the British parliamentary system when a Bill, which has the support of the majority of MPs and the British public, is allowed to be wrecked by a minority in Parliament. It was also a sad day for the Labour Government which, by not giving time to the Bill, not only allowed their fellow Labour Members of Parliament who supported the Bill to be humiliated, but betrayed the trust of the British people who believed that a Labour Government would live up to its often stated commitment, made whilst in opposition, to bring an end to all hunting with dogs.

Michael Fosters Bill was not just about ending animal cruelty, it was also about standards of decency and civilised behaviour. Hunting with dogs is brutal, barbaric and is a relic of the dark ages which should take its rightful place alongside bear/badger-baiting and dog fighting which are illegal. Recent press speculation suggests that as a result of public and parliamentary disquiet over the failure of the *Wild Mammals (Hunting With Dogs) Bill* to become law, Government ministers have been meeting with Labour MPs and others to resurrect legislation in the next session of Parliament to outlaw hunting with dogs. What is certain, however, is that the end to this barbaric practice is tantalisingly close and, when the end does come, something very unpleasant will have been removed from our way of life.

26th August 1998

Gordon Meade

North of Normal

after Edward Summerton

Our shaman keeps
His second skin inside
An open sardine tin.

He wraps a fish
Within a shroud just to confuse
The puzzled crowd.

He pins a crow's head
On a knife just to remind us
There is a point to life.

He spikes an oakleaf
On a thorn to tell us we all have
To die in order to be born.

He nails a catherine wheel
Through a white asbestos glove to show us
The beauty and the price of love.

A Pair of Snowy Owls

Neither out on a limb, nor silhouetted
Against a northern moon, but down amongst
The leaf litter on a cage floor,

Yet all the more striking in spite
Of it all; the white-out of a blank page;
Of a searchlight shone full in the face;
Of Lot's wife after God's blind rage.

The calls from him to her are comic;
An asthmatic love; the whirr of a broken-.
Down fan; the starting motor of a clapped-
Out van; a bronchial sort of passion.

And in the end, they are not for
His partner, but for the dead rat he has
Just uncovered. It seems that for those
Who have lost the need to kill,

The pleasure lies neither in the chase,
Nor in the hunter's skill, but merely
In the act of being filled.

Spectre of the Sea

after Adolph Gottlieb

Looking through this glass-
Bottomed boat is like looking through
A stained-glass window into

The cathedral of the sea.
The face, that stares back at you,
Like that of any drowned man,

Is inscrutable; and the single eye,
Hovering above it, is both omniscient
And blind. Suddenly, you find

Yourself surrounded by creatures
Of the deep. Their sunken reef is made
Up from varying shades of green

And black. Here, there is no
Difference between plenitude and lack.
As you batter bruised and bloody

Fists against reinforced glass,
You slowly come to realise, there is only
One way through and no way back.

Symbols of Survival

after Will Maclean

It is there

in the grain,
in the carved,
polished wood.

It is there

in the rolled
canvas apron, in the open
pockets of pine.

It is there

in the harpoons,
in the pork-rind, in the printed
instructions.

The life

of the imagination
survives everything,
even the skull

of a porpoise.

Composite Memory (Vessel)

After Will Maclean

It is cut

through

the hold

Of a ship;

a cross-

section;

An unnatural

disorder;

a jumble.

A ship

of fools;

a ship

Of death;

a ship

of emigrants,

Wrecked.

An empty

vessel;

A nation's

composite

memory.

J. N. Reilly

Extracts from
Magnificent Despair
a mystery story

… I couldn't care less. It's more than my job's worth. If I lost my job
I couldn't find another. I'm here to shred every single sheet given to
me. I make tea when I'm told to. I take appointments. I write them in
the appointment book then feed them to the computer. My job doesn't
seem important, but it is to me. What do you do? You haven't told me
what you do. Are you doing something more worthwhile? Something
for society…

… the telephone ringing – curtains tremulous in a soft breeze – surf
splashing the beach – a ship in the offing – a postcard and notebook
lying on the table…

… he poured another glass of whiskey for himself and went over to
the window. His gaze was instantly possessed by the gable-end across
the street on which something had been written in Arabic, or was it
Arabic?, in red paint, the paint conspicuously still wet as drips were
slowly trickling from some of the letters of this exquisitely cursive
calligraphy, which fascinated him even as he looked up and down the
street, as if searching for the culprit…

… at the verge of darkness – naked hearts – handfuls of cunt – the
spells of drums – oh to be in Scotland – smoking black…

... he looked at the clock on the wall. It was 8 p.m. He picked the magazine from amongst other magazines on the table. The cover photograph was of a beautiful girl on a sandy beach, palm trees to her right and the ocean to her left. Topless, she was wearing red bikini pants, and seemed to be smiling directly at him. At the top of the magazine something had been written in red ink. He tore the cover from the magazine to pin to the notice-board, and closed his eyes...

... rows of flats, one above the other – a power station – wires against grey – thistle lying in the gutter – it looks like there might be rain – desolate street – boys on the corner...

... strange music – the throb of spring – caged hearts singing – a dog barking – semen dripping from the branches of a naked black tree – the sun red...

... sitting on a black leather couch, the supervisor watched the screen. His wife handed him a glass of red wine. He felt listless, though permeated with the contentment of a good day's work satisfactorily completed. He watched a white ship cutting through deep blue sea, then changed channel. It was not yet dark, though it was late. His wife moved closer to him and began caressing the nape of his neck. She told him that two envelopes and a postcard had been delivered...

... two men in black – at the verge of death – harbour lights dripping into the water – they played cards – looking for conviction – the evidence of codes – handfuls of skin...

... the Corporation disseminates its own texts and finances the dissemination of texts by freelancers who see themselves as responsible contributors due rewards for their contribution to the System. They are viewed as scrambling devices by the Corporation, crutches for the System they believe benefits them, indeed the System is so awash with texts, of which many are connected with the Corporation though more with the System, that the supervisor knows his job is unnecessary...

... someone had written something in a strange calligraphy in red ink across the magazine's cover photograph which was of a leafless black tree with a photograph at the end of a length of rope, maybe even wire, attached to one of its branches, a thick lower branch. He could not distinguish what the photograph was of, because it was small. He tore the cover from the magazine to pin it to the notice-board. He looked at the clock on the wall...

... indians dancing – red spells dripping letters – blue codes merging with pictures – white sailing at the verge of silence – morning sounds sizzling...

... the System is a code; protean. The System has value only in that it is a code. Codes are messages. What is a code? A code is a grimy sheet of newspaper blown along a rainy night street neon flashing...

... two men in black. Photographs behind them, colour photographs, one of which was of a corridor, implicative of an officious building. I did not see any doors, or an end...

... oh to be in Scotland – apple-blossom prayer rising from eternal shores – serene islands afloat – shells and visions of wilderness – sumptuous azure trickling...

... sweetheart, I smuggled visions, prayers, sacraments of quotidian exaltation hallucinated through customs. They want my extinction. They still believe they can destroy I. But they have left it too late, for I am immortal, satellites are receiving and transmitting...

July 1985

Willy Slavin

Whit A State!

For the Scot abroad being misidentified as English or, possibly worse, American is an irritating hazard. Insisting on one's true origins however is likely to lead to a better reaction. A quick association with Scotch – the liquor, not the people – usually means smiles all round. An imaginary glass is raised. Whisky is such a powerful stimulant that even the thought of it can serve as a useful icebreaker.

It is probably the most powerful psychoactive substance (*or drug*) ever licensed by any government. The uninitiated who sat down to drink a bottle of it would be dead before it was finished. It only survived in the Highlands because the Hanoverian military couldn't get over the mountains quickly enough to destroy the stills. The marketing of today's *Whisky Heritage Trail* would have struck as richly ironic the smugglers who braved persecution to pioneer it. Whisky's rehabilitation from *poteen* to a mainstay of the Scottish economy has been gradual. Only in recent years, for example, has it been OK to market it among younger people.

It is all the more bizarre, therefore, that the Scotch (as we used to be called) are so prominent in the so-called *war against drugs*. The police and, even more so, Customs and Excise, seem full of Scots. And now so too is the Cabinet. What chance therefore of a new drugs policy from New Labour?

We need to own our past, as they say. The psychoactive substances that we are most familiar with – *our favourite drugs* as they are now called – are the ones that have been prolifically manufactured and aggressively advertised in our midst. They are, of course, tobacco, alcohol and the pharmaceutical products – fags, booze and pills. Anyone from seventeenth century Scotland where even tea and coffee were ridiculed and persecuted as devilish potions would be amazed to see how many powerful substances have been domesticated, as it were, and distributed through mass production.

The humble cigarette, for example, has long been held up as a brilliant instance of western technology. It contains hardly a milligram of the drug *nicotine* yet, because of the way it is packaged and delivered, it has become as natural to some as sucking is to a child. Western governments, with their usual efficiency, have insisted on the highest standards for the drugs they license. As health beyond mere survival has become important to us, health warnings on all products, including drugs, have become more prominent. Governments also heavily tax domestic drugs and successive Chancellors of the Exchequer have consistently moved towards raising these so that tax revenue can compensate for the more malign effects of the nation's drug habits.

For the people's pleasure does not come without cost. Firstly there are the ever spiralling levels of consumption of all psychoactive substances starting with sugary sweets and fizzy drinks among very young children. We have become wealthy enough to afford a culture in which pain is often smothered even before its signals have been recognised. The goal is *a pill for every ill.* This year's NHS anniversary stamp boasts that, after 50 years of the Health Service, 1,750,000 prescriptions are being dispensed daily. One can hardly grieve publicly for a relative or friend but somebody is urging one to go to the doctor "to get something". In the blackspots of unemployment every corner shop (and the ones in between) have a liquor license and specialise in the ciders and fortified wines that the poor can afford. Demands for Viagra by better off men are now threatening to bankrupt some health boards!

In addition to the rising levels of general consumption there are the problems of compulsive consumption or *addiction.* The majority of cigarette smokers believe they cannot give up the habit. They talk about "dying for a fag" and there are times when they say they could kill for one. In most indices of ill-health, including homelessness and violence, it is increasingly recognised that an addiction to alcohol is often a complicating factor. As for the pills, GPs probably spend as much time persuading some to take them as they do with others persuading them to stop. No matter how much one disapproves of the foolhardiness of the weekend clubbers who blindly ingest the performance enhancing pills concocted by do-it-yourself chemists, nobody is accusing them of being addicted.

It is into this economy sparkling with the conspicuous consumption of psychoactive substances where there is also a significant minority addicted to drink, smoking or to pills that there has come in the last generation and from other countries increasingly loud rumours of new and, it is alleged, better ways of getting a buzz or a rush. And no need to be sick all over your good suit or to smash up the furniture. For these new drugs promise instant inebriation. For a population that no longer has time to enjoy the brewing of coffee, that gets its dinner out of the fridge but has time and money for expanding its leisure and pleasure it sounds just what the doctor ordered. The only drawback is that these are *foreign substances* from far away places with strange sounding names.

Those that have become best known to us are cannabis, heroin and cocaine. They have really only come into our ken through post-war immigration, holidays abroad and the globalisation of the market with all the enhancements that TV lends to these. Marijuana, for example, in the form of *ganga* was popular with some of the immigrants who were invited from the Caribbean to supplement the post-war labour market. In 1967 it decorated the sleeve of the Beatles' most popular record, *Sgt Pepper's Lonely Hearts Club Band*. In 1992 the first US President to have confessed to smoking pot was elected to office.

Cocaine has found it more difficult to make the long journey from South America to Scotland and it still retains some of the mystique of a "champagne drug" favoured by the better off. Heroin, however, with all its Middle East connections has managed to secure a niche in our psychoactive market. In the 1970s it was necessary to go down to the so-called *witchdoctors* in Harley St. to buy private prescriptions but since the 1980s it has become available in most Scottish streets. It has acquired a reputation for being the *best bang for the buck.* The most economical way to use it is by injection, the preferred route of ingestion by those who cannot afford to blow any of it away in smoke.

It is among these poor *smack* (heroin) injectors that reports of the negative effects of drugs have been concentrated. It appears to be forgotten that they are part of that minority which has been unable to cope with our own domestic drugs. Most of them confess to finding it impossible to give up cigarettes even when they are off heroin! Many will recall a family history of alcohol abuse and some are more familiar with the NHS drug formulary than their GP. The reason that heroin appears to be even worse for them lies in the circumstances of its consumption. First of all it is marketed very poorly and it is often of quite uneven quality. Also it has to be consumed in secret with all the risks that any solitary habit brings.

It is this that is the strange thing. One would have thought that the commercial brains that have succeeded in keeping tobacco in business despite cancer and which are able to promote a cool image of alcohol despite all the violence, would have been able to do as much and more with cannabis and heroin. But it appears not. Of course they have other priorities. Recruiting young (tobacco) smokers is no longer as easy as it was. There are restrictions beginning to be imposed on drinking. But these industries have enormous resources and one would have thought they would have been using some of them to examine the market possibilities of the psychedelic experiences that the youth of today are experimenting with.

But at this point that otherwise normal conversation changes tune. Words like drugs cease to mean what they have always meant (a psychoactive substance inducing an altered state of mind – e.g. tea) and start to mean something different e.g. demonic. For when we talk about tobacco, alcohol and the pharmaceuticals the language is strictly of the market. Give the people what they want! The customer knows best! No government should interfere with our natural appetites! On the other hand, however, it is just enough to mention the words *cannabis, heroin and cocaine* and the devil becomes incarnate in our midst.

And yet, oddly enough, it is about the effects of tobacco and alcohol that we know most. The cancer wards are full of the victims of one and the criminal courts with the abusers of the other. Everyone in Scotland knows family or friends who have suffered because of these. In comparison relatively little knowledge can be gleaned about cannabis and heroin. But does this inhibit judges, doctors and teachers (to mention only those who should know best) from pontificating about their *evil* effects? Not a bit of it. Every day we have to listen to a litany of woe about what will happen if these demons get a chance to infect our society. It is as if they were wild beasts lying in wait to grab out innocent children by the throat and force addiction upon them.

It is hard to know exactly where this nonsense comes from. One can respect those who from a religious tradition or an otherwise abstemious background advocate total prohibition or even temperance for health's sake. But the majority of people are probably just victims of the law of inertia. They accept the conventional wisdom as formed by education, medicine and the law. But the average punter also knows that times change and we have to change with them. There has been in the last generation a most significant expansion in the repertoire of drugs available. For once the response has not been economic adaptation but moral condemnation.

It is now 15 years since I first saw in a Scottish prison a case of heroin intoxication. Like all the other observers I presumed it was the usual DTs resulting from alcohol abuse. Had it been booze the young man would in all likelihood still be alive today. Because it was heroin he died a couple of years later injecting in an empty flat above his mother's. Since then hundreds of other young Scots have died in similarly pathetic circumstances. How comes it that drugs which have such similar effects are treated so differently in Scotland today? The distinction between *soft* and *hard* drugs is clearly artificial.

I have come to the conclusion that ultimately the only convincing reason is good old fashioned racism, fuelled by Europe's imperial legacy combined with the present domination of the global economy by the United States. In brief: nothing is to be allowed to compete with the West's control of the enormous global market in tobacco, alcohol and pills. In a way you have to admire the entrepreneurial cheek by which British American Tobacco (*sic*) is trying to penetrate the enormous Chinese cigarette market. Especially if you remember the Opium Wars of the last century when Britain actually went to war in China because the Emperor threw into the sea the opium the British were trying to sell to the Chinese! Even today the muslim prohibition on alcohol that affects a significant number of countries is not something that western countries intend to be limited by. And of course the whole of the Third World provides a useful dumping ground for the pills that are no longer current in the West.

From this perspective it can be seen that the liberal debate about decriminalisation of the new drugs is mostly academic. It is the intention of the industrialised nations to keep Third World drugs commercially non-viable. Indeed the United States has embarked on a programme to eradicate crops natural to these countries. The irony of Third World debt is that if they were allowed to sell their psychoactive substances at prices comparable to whisky (mostly Scottish water) they would be well able to pay their own way! Cannabis, for example, has long had a sacred place in Rastafarian rites. The coca leaf has refreshed the Bolivian tin miner for generations. Opium is such an effective painkiller because it mimics so closely the body's natural endorphins.

Interestingly the UK has held on to the right to dispense heroin and cocaine medically. Surprisingly the relatively mild cannabis lost the right to be prescribed due to an anomaly in UN law by which it was erroneously categorised as a narcotic. So a good place to start changing our attitude to drugs would be to join in the growing campaign to restore the right of medical access to cannabis. A slight change towards acceptance in this direction can already be detected even in the punitive Scottish courts.

This small step to rehabilitate cannabis as a medicine would have a wider effect. It would be a significant crack in the composure of the so-called anti-drugs lobby whose campaigns are politically restricted to the substandard products that are smuggled in from overseas. At least we wouldn't have to listen any longer to silly drugs officers telling incredulous schoolboys that their genitals will atrophy if they take hash. We might instead observe football supporters who have demonstrated that hash is amore peaceful accompaniment to the match than alcohol.

It would be encouraging at least to hear a different tone from New Labour, especially after the new Home Secretary's son was set up in a minor hash deal by an unscrupulous reporter. But to date the old Tory rhetoric is intact. As in the US our criminal system is heading for a complete choke-up despite the commissioning of private jails. This is almost entirely due to the zealous pursuit of those who prefer foreign drugs. The dangers of our own domestic drugs are relegated to the antics of an idiotic minority who are no longer worth bothering about apparently. Nary a prosecution for the widespread disregard of the laws against selling nicotine to under 16s while the murder of pedestrians by drunken drivers still attracts a slap on the wrist.

Some years ago I was invited down to London to meet some Columbian clergy at a conference comparing the effects of drugs on poor communities in Europe and in South America. Imagine how gobsmacked the audience was when one priest described how, when the coca deals were completed and the cash handed over, what their villagers then looked for in order to celebrate their "export" success was, naturally, an exotic foreign substance: viz. Scotch! That was when, he said, the mayhem really started, the guns came out and people got "sorted". As the Bard said: *Would the gods the giftie gie us tae see oursels as others see us.*

31 August 1998

Dee Rimbaud

An Unbearable Ecstasy

I can't exactly say it always happens, coz this is only the second time, but already I feel like saying, "it always happens". It's like I never learn. The first time I did E was with a pill head lassie I fell in love with almost instantaneously. Didn't know it was a chemical trick. She fucked my head about something rotten. And I still love her. There's a bit of her in my bloodstream. It just gets pumped round in weird mooncycles and spins through my heart every now and then. It's not exactly predictable. It just happens. I haven't seen her in ages.

Thought I'd never do E again, but here I am, and I have. Neil says it's mostly speed, but I'm feeling the same hot rush we got off of that stuff that I broke my E virginity with, and he claimed that that was "pure". I don't know. I think he's on some sort of initiating the old codger trip. Gets off on it. Teaching his grandfather how to fuck with drugs.

Anyway, here I am in some sweatpit club again, falling in love again, out of my face on E again. Vowed I'd never do any of these things again. But here I am. I never learn.

Started coming up in the taxi. Too early. Fun taxi ride, like. But I'd rather be doing the soaring now. Got really fucking edgy in the queue. Crowds and waiting oppress me. I need space, you know? And it's too crowded in here and all. These club owners have no spirit. We're just cattle. Eight quid a head. Cram 'em in. Maybe the vibe's shit. Just like the last time.

59

But now I'm thinking too much about it all. I came to dance. That's all I want to do. Let this drug take me to that other place. I mean, I'm dancing, I'm really moving, but it isn't with soul. D'you know what I mean? Last time, with Rina, it was with soul. Like we were dancing into each others eyes. And everything else dissolved into nothing. Felt like singing that song "I only have eyes for you". Shite song, like, but I know now what it was all about. We could have been anywhere. It was too good. Rina, what a heart and head fuck. I really opened up my gate to her. Like I was a teenager again. And she went in and ransacked my garden with her hard-bitch-with-attitude mask and stiletto jackboots. You'd think I'd learn. But here I am, loved up and in love again. And I vowed, never again.

Her name is Lorraine. She's got a shy wee smile and frightened rabbit eyes. She looks kind of lost in this place. Her mates are whooping it up, standing on the platform, waving their arms like spassies. All of them in these shiny black dresses. All tits and lipstick. Fuck knows what they're on. Fuck knows what they're looking for. Get a really desperate vibe off of them. Get the same vibe off of my wee Lorraine, but she's different, you know? She doesn't pull off the act like the others. The wee clingy dress is like a straight jacket on her. She's all constrained, like, not into the dancing at all, not even pretending very well. They've all got the big black pupils, all out of their faces. But she's not out of anything. Looks like she wants to cry. And I really want to give her a big hug or something. Except, I feel kind of constrained myself. Just not up enough. If I could get hold of another pill, maybe.

I get back from the toilet, and there's no sign of Lorraine. All her daft pals are there, but not her. And I'm feeling pretty bummed out now. Waiting for "a table for one" in the toilets (coz I never can go, standing at one of these metal troughs like a fucking animal), I overhear these skinhead guys, and one of them says to the other, "So, you gonna shag that wee slag?" "Fuck, no her, she's a fucking dog, it's the one with the tits ahm eftir" replies the other. When I get into the cubicle, it's a long time before I can go. I hear a succession of guys enter and leave. They all speak in harsh tones. Like walk-ons from "Trainspotting". And all they talk about is who they're going to fuck, and what drugs they've taken. And I'm so desperate to piss and just get out of there I just can't go. I feel like a middle-class wanker trapped in a hell he just can't comprehend. And I keep thinking about these lassies I've been looking at all night. It doesn't matter how hard they seem on the surface, all I can see is their softness, their neediness. And I think about the arseholes who are going to fuck them tonight. And I kind of really hurt for them.

When I get back to the dance-floor, there's no Lorraine, and no way I can dance. The music's turned to shit, and it's so fucking loud I can't breathe.

The "chill out zone" is an alcove off the bar where you can hear the music from both dance floors, and folk can just about talk if they shout. It's not exactly pleasant, but it's better than hanging out on the dance-floor with my ears bleeding.

I bump into Neil and Elaine. They're sitting at the edge of one of the overcrowded tables. I've sat down beside them before I realise they're having a domestic. Elaine is calling Neil all the wankers under the sun, and he's smiling away like crazy and keeps saying, "But it's like this..." Except he never gets a chance to say what it's like. I sit and drink Elaine's cider until she gets up and goes off. "Fuck, man, women..." says Neil, winking in what he must imagine is complicity. I think about just getting a taxi home, but then I think about Lorraine again. I leave Neil and go back to the dance-floor to look for her. I don't know what exactly I want. I mean, the last thing I want right now is a fuck. I guess I just want to be around her, to fend off the wolves, you know?

I find her and she looks fucking awful. Her face is green. And it's not the lighting. Something sort of happens inside me and I just reach over and take her hand, stroke her fingers and look into her eyes. Her eyes look really desperate and sad. I ask her if she wants to leave, and she says she does. I mean, we've hardly said fuck all to each other all night. All I know is she's called Lorraine and she's from Muirhouse. That's it. Just something clicked between us. And maybe it is just the E, but who gives a fuck?

We go look for our jackets and then make our way to the exit. I pass Neil on the way out, and he shouts out, "You score, man? Fucking go for it." I tell him to fuck off. "Chill man, you know? I was just saying..." he says.

When we get out the club I feel like I can breathe again. The wind coming up off the Forth makes me feel kind of invigorated. I want to just pick Lorraine up and run off with her, you know? But she's kind of unsteady on her pins. We cut up some stairs off the Cowgate, and before we get half way she collapses in a wee heap and starts puking. I get down beside her, and just start stroking her back. I almost feel like saying "there there". When she's finished, she gets up and pulls a bog roll out of her hand bag and starts dabbing shakily at her mouth. "Is it all away?" she asks. I take some bog roll off her and clean her up some more. I feel like a fucking mother.

We get up the stairs onto Chamber Street and begin the fruitless task of looking for a taxi. Us and several dozen other disappointed looking clubbers. "It's a long walk to Muirhouse" I say to her. "Ah dinnae want to go back there, ah want tae go to yours." she says.

So we walk out to mine. My nice wee flat in Newington. "Ahm fucked," she says, when we get in the door, "where's the bedroom?" I point her in the right direction, then go off to the kitchen to make up some teas and dig out the jaffa cakes. When I get into the bedroom she's lying in bed with her tits hanging over the duvet like an offering. I get the vibe, straight off that she thinks there's an automatic price for my hospitality. I just try to ignore it, but I'm kind of trembling inside, and there's a wee lust demon tickling me downstairs. "Like a wee lamb to the slaughter" I find myself thinking. I give her the tea and the packet of jaffa cakes and run round the room, sorting the ambience. I light a couple of incense sticks and some candles and dig out my tape of "Protection" by Massive Attack. Perfect come down music. I sit down on the edge of the bed, feeling a bit uncomfy. "This is a barry flat," she says, "is it all yours, like?" I tell her it's my mother's and her eyes go kind of wide. "What? You live with your mum?" So, I explain to her that my mother bought it for me, and I can just feel my cheeks burning up: hoping to fuck she can't see it in the candlelight. She doesn't say anything to that, just "you going to get in or what?"

I get undressed and get in under the duvet. Then she just sort of opens her legs and waits for me. This embarrasses me no end. "Listen," I say, after a silence that's just too long, "I don't want to fuck, you know? I just want to cuddle." She looks at me, all confused, like... I don't know. "It's not like I don't fancy you or anything," I say, but I think I just add to her confusion.

At first we are a bit clumsy with each other, but then we kind of end up lost in kissing and stroking each other. And before I know it, the sweet sounds of Shara Nelson's voice are buzzing round my head and I'm down between Lorraine's legs, licking her like crazy. And the taste of her makes me dizzy. She starts squeaking and oo-ing, like a broken doll, and then she yanks me up and I'm inside her.

I move inside her really slowly, protracting the moment until it's an unbearable ecstasy. And when we come, it's like a dying sigh. We just melt together.

After a while we sort of slip apart. I kiss her some then slip behind her, put my arm round her, and pull her into my protection. Like a big mother.

She yawns, stretches into me and mumbles, "you're the nicest fellie ahv ever met." I watch over her as she slips into sleep, feeling the mounting panic rise up inside me.

Graham Fulton

Froth
Amsterdam, 1991

Skinshow gangsters,
last night's dross.

Pushers wait in
whisper cafés,
sniff the takings,
suck
    up
        froth.

The prostitutes
have gone home
to rest before
the evening shift

feed their children
fish fingers,
tales about
a princess blowing
pink-lit kisses,
hair
    thrown
        down.

A clanking tram
hurls and sparks
towards the heart
of Amsterdam.

Whip-shop dummies,
needled veins.
Doorway beds,
boiling brains.

Junkies stand in
bloodsplash alleys,
scream at tulips,
count
    their
        hands.

Pleasure Hormones Race

On a Brooklyn Burgh waste ground,
screened from the freeway by tall old trees,
five workers, negro, young, dig
a pit
six feet deep, twenty long, ten wide. Distant

towers shimmer

in haze. The sun
is hot for the
time of year.
Magnificent high, to the brain,
ten seconds, all it takes,
shovels flash, dirt flies up,
steady work, a small wage. Everyone

tries to ease

the pain. Pleasure.
hormones race to the brain. A van
is parked four yards away, the driver
checks the baseball scores, the back
is big, inside are stacked
three hundred boxes filled

with babies

born, soon dead, hooked on crack.
A number in chalk on each tidy box
to keep the records up to date.
Magnificent high, crack cocaine,
all it takes, fill the space,
New York Times, smooth the soil,
buy the food, pay the rent. Another

van is next to that, another

next to that
as Manhattan's barons snooze in shade.
No-one talks. Burying waste,
close your heart, all it takes.
Pleasure hormones to the brain.
Drag the rakes, leave no

trace.

There's Nothing There

there's nothing there
that wasn't there
before
it's just
the end of this
liquid thunder
in the head
listening to
the end of this
absence
birth chords
bedlam tunes
an orchestra
of lunatics

is
soothing
deep

there's nothing
there
that wasn't there
before
it's just
the absence of light
familiar points
of reference
just
the absence
of familiar objects
wardrobe
chair
fingers
toes

the green glow
of the bedside
clock
clicking
from number
to number
one
past
four

is soothing
deep
there's nothing
there
that wasn't

it's just
the sound
of everything
all you know
being left behind
the rhythm is flawed
try to explode
all you know
tinfoil
ringpulls
human left-overs
animal syrup
bones and crumbs
ribs and spit
round and round
cosy monsters
in and out
the beat is flawed
the heart is flawed
the cold
the heart of everything
love

musty books
on bookcase shelves
heart of darkness
moby dick
with best wishes
from Uncle Jock
Christmas 1932
dry
familiar
father
dust
mother
home
all you know
familiar points
of reference
just
flowers pressed
between
the pages

sitting alone
on soft
sweat crushed
velvet stools
in lost soul bars
smiling
as the days
fly
off

with all
the things
that will never
be said
all
the things
that will never

be done
all
the ghosts
you half-glimpse
out the corner
of your eye
as you wait
at bus stops
counters
checkouts
bus stops
as you wait
to pay your bill

or
stand
in the lift
the red light
jumping
number to
number
four to five
bags full
of shopping
fish
fingers
drink
potatoes
all you know
human breathing
sound
of nothing
father
mother
country roads
the cable snapping
take me home
rush through space

is soothing
deep
sleep
sound
there's nothing there

that wasn't there
before
it's just

Louise Cockburn

Tuition Fees? No, No, No Tony!

A New Caring Sharing Britain?

Labour under Tony Blair have been in government for a little over a year yet this new caring face of Britain has been shown to be a mere façade. On May 1st. "Middle England" rejected the Tories thereby giving Britain the first Labour government in eighteen years. But have things "only got better"? The answer is clearly in the negative – what we are witnessing is a Government swept to power on a manifesto which has been ignored in order to curry favour with the privileged few. Any principles of egality have conveniently been forgotten yet we are still expected to believe that New Labour cares. Perhaps one of the most glaring examples of New Labour's contempt for the people they are meant to serve is the introduction of tuition fees and the abolition of maintenance grants from the next academic year. To use a well-worn cliché in student circles this is "Labour's Poll Tax on Education".

As If Things Are Not Bad Enough.

Contrary to popular belief students these days are not beer-swilling, drunken louts who see the inside of a lecture theatre only at the start of their first year. Due to the cuts levelled by the Tories on the maintenance grant, to enable themselves to eat, four out of ten students are employed during term times and 66% work during vacations. The jobs which students perform are mainly low-paid with abominable conditions – over 80% of students employed during term times receive no sick pay or holiday pay and approximately 40% are not entitled to either meal or tea breaks. Whilst many people are forced to be subjected to dreadful working conditions students are meant to be studying for a better future of employment conditions thereby contributing to society by paying taxes proportional to their higher rates of pay. Unfortunately due to the pressures of combining working and studying an estimated 4,752 left courses prematurely in Scotland in 1994/5 which is a rise of 10% on the figures for 1993/4. Thus society is not benefiting from the potential increase in revenue derived from the taxation system. In addition two thirds of the students who work during term times said that their employment had detrimentally affected their studies with over 30% missing lectures and 20% failing to submit work due to their having no choice but to work to survive. If the figures are horrendous now one hesitates to imagine what they will be like when the new proposals come into effect.

New Labour. New Taxes.

The reality is that Blair and his henchmen have succeeded in killing the long-standing and popular principle of "Free Education". Even Thatcher failed in her attempt to do likewise – in 1984 she tried to introduce tuition fees of £400 per annum. Even she did not dare to suggest the abolition of grants.

However thirteen years later Blair has succeeded in imposing a new tax which is more than double that mooted by the Tories. He has even abolished grants – no longer will students receive the essential pittance from the Government. Not content to stop there the Islington

Coterie have cut spending on centrally-funded education by 10% - "a triple whammy on education".

New Labour. New Centralisation.

Education will be devolved to the Scottish Parliament. Given that the minister who imposed these draconian measures has made it clear that his future remains at Westminster we should consider the funding of education only when the Scottish Parliament is up and running. He has obviously no interest in Scottish education and therefore he should be prevented from implementing proposals which do not command the support of the Scottish people and he does not consider to be important enough to interest him. Indeed in a recent poll in "Scotland On Sunday" (20th July) 75% of Scots oppose tuition fees. It seems that these proposals are being pushed through before the Parliament comes into existence, by an uncaring anti-Scottish government, since they are only too aware that these proposals would not be endorsed by a Scottish Parliament. Really, Mr. Wilson should grow up.

To add insult to injury we now find that Helen Liddell is to oversee these proposals' implementation. Another member of Blair's clique, Mrs. Liddell has been sent home to "hammer the Nats". During the Monklands by-election, this "hammer" promised to sort out the sleaze in what is now called North Lanarkshire. She still has not done so; even if the Council has been renamed, nepotism and sleaze remain the predominant factors of political life in North Lanarkshire and every Labour controlled council for that matter. Mrs. Liddell should concentrate on hammering out Labour's rotten core instead of criticising a party whose sole aim is to improve the lives of everyone, not just the privileged few. However that is a marathon task and Labour's chosen few want to continue living in splendour. What are ideals and principles anyway? Certainly New Labour have never held them in high regard!

The Poll Tax On Education.

So what are Labour's proposals? Firstly, students starting their degree next year will have to pay £1,000 for the privilege of studying at university. Secondly, only those students currently in Higher

Education will receive a grant. Labour in their no-substance sound-bites assert that there is a threshold to ensure that only those who can afford to pay will pay. In any event what guarantee do we have that the threshold will be maintained at a reasonable level? Interestingly, the Republic of Ireland, so long pitied by the UK as our poor relation, has just abolished tuition fees. By the year 2000, Eire will be richer than the UK. This can almost certainly be attributed in part to the huge emphasis placed on education by successive Irish Governments. The irony is not lost when we consider that Eire copied the Scottish Education system when looking to improve the wealth of the Emerald Isle.

Why We Must Stop These Proposals From Being Implemented.

This is an issue which has united all those involved in education – students, lecturers, and university principals are vehemently opposed to this deeply unjust, prejudicial and socially divisive measure. Using figures from Brian Wilson it is apparent that these plans will hit students from poorer backgrounds the hardest. Around 43% will be exempted from paying the fees because their parents earn less than the £23,000 threshold. "Great" some might say. However if one looks at the grim realities the picture looks less than rosy. (No pun intended!). A student who does not pay the tax will leave university with debts totalling £13,760. If one then assumes that the parental income is £23,000 over four years this amounts to £92,000. Thus the debt incurred is 14.9% of the parental income.

It is even worse for the average Scot. Figures from the New Earnings Survey (Office For National Statistics) show that the average Scot receives £16,894.80 in wages each year. Thus the proportion of student debt to the parental income is a staggering 20.4%. Contrast that with the figures for those who have to pay the fees. The relative percentage here is "only" 9.8%. In fact students from well-off backgrounds will incur a smaller debt.

The only reasonable conclusion that can be drawn from these figures is that the Government is taxing the poor to pay for the rich – some things never seem to change regardless of what party is in power at Westminster.

These figures are not lost on students and potential students. With increasing graduate unemployment – currently at 10.6% compared to the national average of 8.5% fewer people will be willing to take on this enormous burden of debt. Under New Labour society will be regressing to the era where only the rich can attend university. So much for the classless society Tony!

Education-Only Free With The SNP

Unlike the other political parties the SNP values the young, seeing them as the future of our country. We do not believe in short-term measures. We are the only party which would re-introduce grants, restore benefits during the vacations and give housing benefit to students. We are firmly in favour of these policies because we are of the opinion that "Free Education" benefits society as a whole, because anything less is frankly unacceptable. Through a progressive taxation system those students who go on to earn large salaries would obviously pay slightly more thereby benefiting society generally. The "I'm all right Jack" attitude fostered by the last Tory government is alive and flourishing during the tenure of this alternative Tory government. It is not surprising therefore that society in Britain lacks cohesion and respect for others leading to rising crime, poverty and the resulting misery for the vast majority of the population.

. Therefore on May 6th 1999 Scotland must show London Labour that we are not prepared to tolerate socially exclusive measures. We want a fair and just society, where people care for each other, not just themselves. That's why the first Scottish Parliament in nearly 300 years will have a huge SNP presence at the very least. If opinion polls are correct it is likely that the SNP will be in power. And what better way to show the rest of the world that we Scots are a mature and forward-looking bunch who are ready, willing and able to make the world a better place for everyone?

Freddy Anderson

Samizdat Literature In Scotland From Burns Onwards

'Samizdat', a Russian word, now used internationally to describe the clandestine publication and distribution of any banned or dissident literature. Scotland, particularly the West Coast, has had a very rich seam of samizdat in both literature and song. As Capitalism becomes increasingly decadent and archaic, this form of angry protest and satire is certain to increase enormously in the months and years ahead.

Seemingly paradoxical, the bawdy ballads and songs were the most vital progressive cultural force in Scotland from the Reformation to the era of the French inspired Enlightenment in the last quarter of the 18th Century. The verses in the main rumbustious and crude, too much so for the 'unco-guid' whose grandchildren would, half-a-century later, join with the English middle-classes to impose a stifling morality on the cultural desert that was 'ruled' by that stiff, podgy, little dumpling, Queen Victoria. These early bawdy ballads left little or nothing to the imagination, they were forthright and sometimes contained witty stanzas, enhanced by the lively robust folk tunes of Scotland. Burns certainly did not collect them for their so-called 'vulgarity'. He knew perfectly well that they were a powerful, virile antidote against the paralysing poison of Calvinist dogma and, indeed, even lesser forms of pious orthodoxy. These 'wicked' ditties helped to ensure an endless queue for the well-worn cutty stools in the countless kirks of Scotland.

Robert Burns not only collected them but added his tuppence worth to them with a flamboyant zest. In 1792, he boasts to his jovial friend, John McMurdo of Drumlanrig, "…. I think I once mentioned to you of a collection of Scots Songs I have for some years been making. I send you a perusal of what I have gathered… There is not another copy of the Collection in the world and I should be sorry that any unfortunate negligence should deprive me of what has cost me a good deal of pains..." Some of these bawdy songs, including his own, were of recent composition, but others dated back two centuries and more before the arrival of Burns on the scene. *Peggy Ramsay*, for example, was mentioned in Shakespeare's works. Burns later titled his Collection, *The Merry Muses of Caledonia* and passed it freely among his close friends. The proud claim of the great poet to be the sole possessor of this unique Collection is indeed justified, for these ballads and songs were passed from generation to generation in the *oral* folk tradition, and no-one (except Burns) had collected any substantial quantity in handwritten form. This Collection and, I am sure, others on a much smaller scale, were among the earliest samizdat literature in Scotland and had as their target the professed 'morality' of State and Kirk.

In the 17th Century, Scotland had no prose literature which could equal in volume or polemical tone the great flood of broadsheets and pamphlets printed by the Diggers and Levellers in England. In Scotland the struggle took on a more complex religious form with the Covenanters in bitter confrontation with the Episcopalians, made even more muddled still by the two Royalist factions. The Act of Union with England in 1707 and the sell-out of Scotland by its own Lords; *A parcel o' Rogues* as Burns too kindly called the traitors; made the Land of Wallace and Bruce into a mere tool of London bankers and merchants for the exploitation and extension of a corrupt Empire right into our own century. Robert Burns, of course, was conscious of the political trends of his day, but there were times when the livelihood of his wife and family were threatened and he was forced to use covert samizdat poetry to avoid transportation as a convict like Muir and Palmer, as he admitted in a rhyming Epistle to his literary correspondent, Maria Riddell. That is why *The Tree of Liberty* and *The Jolly Beggars* were not included in his published works until a long time after his death. Patrick Hogg, a modern historian in Literature, claims that there were several other poems of this character by Burns and quotes them in full in his controversial book, *The Lost Poems of Robert Burns*. Patrick Hogg's argument is that these samizdat poems of Burns are still being deliberately excluded from the

Burns canon by the mainly bourgeois 'gurus', as he calls the Burnsian biographers. It seems to me that the issue is still unresolved.

Burns had his successors in the late eighteenth and early nineteenth Centuries, although none of these were on the same peak of poetical genius as Burns. The famous two Paisley poets, Robert Tannahill and Alexander Wilson were contemporaries of Burns but survived him for several years. Both were radical poets, but Wilson especially could be described as typically samizdat. He was jailed in Paisley for lampooning in bitter satire a greedy mill owner and at the end of his jail sentence, the unrepentant poet was to see his 'savage verses' burned publicly at Paisley Cross. This vitriolic satire is aptly called, *The Shark* and was later widely published. Soon afterwards, Wilson emigrated to America and, wonderful to relate, became within a decade or so, one of the two great founders of American ornithology. Tannahill, on the other hand, devoted his exceptional talent mainly to song-writing, emulating the best of Burns and the Scottish tradition. He is best known to-day as the author of that 'hardy annual' at folk concerts and festivals, *The Braes of Baliquidder* or *Will ye go, lassie, go?* with a very slight alteration of words. What retains Tannahill in the samizdat dissident category, however, are poems like his bold and angry anti-war stanzas, *The Recruiting Drum,* with its nausea declared in the very first line, *I hate the drum's discordant sound.* It is to the credit of Paisley's good taste that the lawn in front of the historic Abbey is honoured solely by the large statues of these two very unique Radicals.

Contemporaneous with Burns, Wilson and Tannahill, were others in the east of Scotland, other samizdat authors who made quite a significant contribution to that genre of literature, and like the great ornithologist, Alexander Wilson, became very famous in spheres of activity quite distinct from Literature. Robert Burns, in a letter to Mrs. Dunlop (an early patroness) in 1788, gives a very amusing, graphic description of one of these highly talented men. "... Those (songs) marked T. are the work of an obscure, tippling, but extraordinary body of the name of Tytler: a mortal, who though he drudges about Edinburgh as a common Printer, with leaky shoes, a sky-lighted hat, and knee-buckles unlike as George-by-the-grace-of-God and Solomon-the-son-of-David, yet that same unknown, drunken Mortal is author and compiler of three fourths of Elliot's pompous

Encyclopaedia Britannica…" The epithet 'extraordinary' coming from a genius of the calibre of Burns is surely indicative of Tytler's worth. A minister's son from Forfar, he attended Edinburgh University for a time, rendered himself penniless by an early marriage, compiled and edited almost the entire third edition of the huge Encyclopaedia, got into debt and had to seek sanctuary in the grounds of Holyrood where he invented not only his own printing machine but the first hot-air balloon to be made in these islands. (With himself as sole passenger he made a half-mile flight – chased no doubt by his frantic creditors!)

Our present essay however, is more interested in his printing activities. After Burns left Edinburgh and passed Tytler's songs for publication in George Thomson's *Select Collection of Scottish (sic) Airs,* this versatile man-of-many-parts espoused the cause of Reform and distributed his own samizdat leaflets and placards in the streets of Edinburgh. The alarmed Authorities would have gaoled or transported him along with Thomas Muir of Huntershill and other Friends of the People had Tytler not fled the country and, now declared an Outlaw, found a temporary 'safe house' in Ulster where he ghosted two volumes of Medicine for an Edinburgh doctor before emigrating to America where he founded a newspaper in the infamous town of Salem. An apt title for a future biography of this astonishing, colourful figure would surely be, THE WIZARD OF SALEM.

Before returning to the west of Scotland, where the bulk of radical activities were to be centred for the next two-and-a-half centuries, one cannot pass, without comment, that remarkable revolutionary dynamo, Dr. Robert Watson, born in 1746 in Elgin. His adventures, quite as amazing as those of Tytler or Wilson, have been narrated as recently as 1996 by a fellow townsman, Graham Bain, in a very absorbing book called, *The Thunderbolt of Reason.* Educated at Aberdeen University, Watson emigrated to the West Indies, and then participated in the American War of Independence and survived it, though with many wounds and a permanent limp. He met Washington and other signatories of the famous Declaration. Returning to Britain, he was very active in the radical London Correspondence Society and on a trumped up charge was gaoled for over two years in the Newgate dungeons. He was constantly tailed by Government agents and police spies who had infiltrated the L.C.S. in droves. He escaped to Paris with a price of £400 as a Government reward for his capture. In Paris, he met Tallyrand, Thomas Muir, Wolfe Tone and Napper Tandy. Like Tom Paine, he had a plain bold style of writing and his samizdat literature of revolt seeped back to England and Scotland.

Some years later he settled in Rome and unearthed a huge quantity of the Stuart Papers, letters which covered the Courts of Europe intrigues about the two failed Jacobite Risings of that century. These documents were eagerly purchased by the notorious Lord Castlereagh and are still under seal at Windsor Castle. Among Watson's chief contributions to radical literature are his extracts from the writings of that great Scottish patriot, Fletcher of Saltoun (Salton). His decree of Outlaw was annulled and he returned to London where at the age of 92 he was strangled in his bed at the Blue Anchor Inn in 1838. The mystery of his murder has never been solved.

No genuine literary historian should dare to omit in a survey of Scottish cultural traditions, the powerful influence of the Gaelic, the Highlands and Islands, and to some extent Irish, contribution to the spirit of revolt against repression. Since the combined Norman and Anglo-Saxon invasions of Wales, Ireland and Scotland which began in the 12th century and has continued to this day, the tyrannical domination by the English establishment has, by its imposed Penal Laws, attempted to force the Gaelic culture into a fugitive character. On that account, it has mainly survived in an oral tradition of spirited rebel song and verse. In particular, after the wholesale butchery of the sadistic Williamites at Culloden, there was for three decades a ruthless campaign by fire and sword to obliterate forever, even the slightest remnants of Gaelic culture in Scotland; the kilt, the bag-pipes, the language and song were proscribed by savage laws. Yet, despite this barbaric action, the bards of the Highlands and Islands produced some of the finest poetry and song. Robert Burns, who lived most of his young manhood during the latter years of this wholesale repression, never hesitated in using Gaelic tunes for his best creations e.g. *Rory Dall (Blind Rory)* the air of his most poignant song, perhaps, *Ae Fond Kiss*.

It was in the latter part of that same century, that the early Highland Clearances and the Industrial Revolution forced the landless Scottish Gaels into the weaving sheds and cotton mills of Glasgow and other towns. It was in these lowly quarters that the Mill-owners had their first major confrontation in 1787 with the weavers at Bridgeton when the hireling Militia fired at point-blank range to murder six poor workers. Many samizdat poems and songs have been written about these Calton Martyrs and this first baptism of fire for the Trade Unionists of Scotland. The foremost writer in this genre of literature in Scotland during his life-time was undoubtedly Alexander "Sandy" Rodger (1784-1846), a Drygate weaver, who was most active in all the turbulent scenes in the battle for Trade Union rights and voting Reform in the first half of the 19th century.

An early pinnacle of this struggle was reached in 1820 through the evil machinations of Lords Castlereagh & Sidmouth (the bloodthirsty scoundrels responsible for 'Peterloo' in 1819) when they provoked, with the wily assistance of their paid provocateurs, a premature Insurrection of weavers mainly who were trapped in their attempt to 'capture' the infamous Arms Industry Iron Works at Carronside near Falkirk. None of the Government spies were gaoled, of course, but three brave weavers were hanged and about twenty others transported. Sandy Rodger had been imprisoned in 1819 when the military destroyed the printing machines of the radical newspaper he sub-edited in Glasgow, *The Spirit of the Union*. (Its editor was transported.) Rodger, akin to Brendan Behan in *Borstal Boy* sang taunting songs to his keepers in the Tolbooth.

At the visit of George IV to Edinburgh in 1822, that arch Tory royalist, Sir Walter Scott, not only helped to arrange this servile show-piece of bourgeois buffoonery but wrote some doggerel lines of welcome to the old air, *Carle an the King's com.* Sandy immediately set to work retaining the tune but creating a ribald Rabelaisian version with this scathing chorus throughout :-

> Sawney, noo the King's come,
> Sawney, noo the King's come
> Kneel an kiss his gracious bum
> On your hunkers, lick his fud,
> Sawney, noo the King's come.

> Tell him he is great and good
> And comes of Scottish Royal blood
> Tae your hunkers, lick his fud,

Sawney, noo the King's come.

An' if there's in St. James' Square
Ony *thing* that's fat an' fair,
Treat him nichtly wi' sic ware,
Sawney, noo the King's come.

When he rides Auld Reekie through
Tae bless ye wi' a Kingly view,
Greet him wi' your Gardyloo,
Sawney, noo the King's come!

It was gleefully reported that the sycophantic, so-called 'Great Unknown', Sir Walter Scott, was not at all amused by the mutilation of his loyal lickspittle hymn of praise at the hands of a 'common pleb' or as his bumptious fellow Tory, Burke, described the likes of Rodger and workers in general – the Great Unwashed. Thousands of copies of Rodger's parody were hawked in not only Edinburgh but Glasgow and throughout Scotland and they were also published later in the poet's book, *Stray Leaves,* a very apt title for a collection of samizdat broadsheets. I know of no other author in Britain in the 19th century (except perhaps Shelley in the powerful *Mask of Anarchy*) who could hold a candle to Sandy Rodger in the creation of satire. He had not, admittedly, the same lofty genius as Burns and Swift of the previous century, but then how many in the entire history of international literature even match these two giants of satire.

Rodger's work contained many brilliant, witty couplets in the Scottish dialect, all carrying 'the savage indignation' of the oppressed weavers and the millions of exploited poor. In the hundred and fifty years since his death, in fact, only a half-dozen Scottish writers have felt even remotely near the passionate, justified anger of Rodger at class distinction and persecution. The historical circumstances that placed him as a strong, splendid voice of working-class protest in Scotland, has virtually excluded his work from the countless volumes of the wan, spiritless drivel, masquerading as 'poetry' in pretentious anthologies and magazines right up to our own sad times of bourgeois social and literary decadence. For almost two centuries, the boss class's fear of the plain Truth, (plus their literary menials' fear of the

81

sack), has confined some superb Radical literature to its samizdat role, not to be circulated among our so-called 'superiors' who, indeed, are most in need of conversion to the reality of the slow but sure steam-roller of History, or in their ignorance and greed be buried like the fossils they are in its passing. The very same applies to the spate of crawling pundits, who miscall themselves 'Historians' (by the permission of their brain-washed University 'professors' and 'examiners') who sneeringly declare that Red Clydeside was nothing but a twentieth century 'myth'. These arrogant dunderheads (if they can read, which I doubt,) have obviously not even heard of Rodger or others; else they would know that the Clyde was Red with the blood of working-class Martyrs and the tyrannised poor of Glasgow for two centuries, long before John MacLean gave his Socialist lectures to countless thousands on Glasgow Green and throughout Scotland.

As mentioned earlier, police informers and sinister Government agents provocateurs infiltrated the London Correspondence Society. They did the same in even greater droves in Glasgow, Paisley, and other towns between the years 1816 and 1824. These infernal scoundrels created mayhem. And then quite amazingly, by a miraculous coincidence almost, Lords Castlereagh and Sidmouth, Kirkman Finlay (the tobacco tycoon) and the city treasurer were exposed for the gangsters they were, to the public at large, in a series of samizdat two-penny pamphlets (ten in total) published by Peter Mackenzie, who might well be called the great founder of what is now called investigative journalism in Glasgow. These powerful pamphlets, entitled *The Exposure of the Spy System in Glasgow*, created a political explosion in the city. They sold like hot cakes.

Kirkman Finlay MP., and erstwhile Lord Provost, was driven out of politics into hiding in his ill-gotten Estate at Toward Castle near Dunoon (of Holy Loch infamy), and by that time the Ulster Irish scoundrel Lord Castlereagh had cut his wretched throat. Kirkman Finlay's proud statue which was to be set up for public admiration in George Square was instead sneaked into the shadows of the stairway of the Chamber of Commerce, the powerful rich consortium that controls the 'elected' City Chambers and the fate of Glasgow to this day. The publicly unwanted statue is a fitting symbol of Corruption of both Chambers in those shameful times and our own no better.

Another samizdat poet in the tradition of Rodger was an emigrant Irish pedlar's son, James McFarlan, who was born in Glasgow in 1830 and died of T.B. in 1860. He had only two years of 'education' and is said to have picked up his love of reading and poetry in particular from an old battered volume of Byron's which he found discarded in a ditch when he was scavenging with his father in a cart in the country lanes around Glasgow. This delicate, sensitive poet lived all his too brief life in the alleys of the tenements, but latterly in an attic in the Drygate (an earlier weaving community).

The great twentieth century poet, Hugh Macdiarmid, in condemning virtually all Victorian 'poetry', states that McFarlan is one of the two Scottish poets whose work is worth even mentioning during that long dull reign. Charles Dickens, who gave a reading in the Old Atheneum in Ingram Street, Glasgow, in the mid-century, and the novelist William Thackeray, also had a good opinion of the quality of McFarlan's poetry. Thackeray remarked in the Garrick Club in London that "even Burns himself could not blow the wind out of this man's sails!" He was referring to McFarlan's poem, *The Lords of Labour* (no connection, I assure, with our current parasitic 'Labour' Lords & Baronesses in the so-called 'Upper House'). The magnificent soaring lines of the poem are dedicated not to sham careerists and glory-mongers but to the sons of toil who for all their slavery are no better off. He wrote on many themes of contrast in the city, lashing the rich, snobbish drones. Yet no matter how bitter his attacks against the hypocrites, he strove to retain a high standard of poetic quality. He had a true aesthetic sensitivity. For the reader I will quote a few of my favourite lines from a fine poem he wrote about a poor tenement wife keeping a candlelight vigil in her attic room awaiting the return of her selfish, drunken husband,

"... she stirs not yet.
The night hath drawn its silent stream of stars away
And now the infant streaks of Dawn
Begin to prophecy the day.
She stirs not yet.

O, heart that will unheeding care,
O, heart that will unheed break

How strong the zeal, how deep the Love
That burns for faithless folly's sake."

I think that there are very few poets even among the famous who can match that quality of imagery and phraseology. A pompous Radio BBC Producer told me that he thought McFarlan a third rate poet. I assured him that 99% of the BBC's 'modern' poets (paid handsomely by them) were surely tenth rate in comparison to Rodger and McFarlan. The BBC poets in the main had really nothing to say, and when they moaned their rubbish, the silence afterwards was a boon. McFarlan was buried in a pauper's grave in Anderston, probably bull-dozed in the Glasgow Council's 're-construction' (destruction, rather) of the old Village

A mere two decades elapsed between the poet's death and the birth of the great Socialist, John MacLean. A future essay will describe samizdat literature in Scotland from MacLean to the present day.

J. N. Reilly

On Crossing the Monklands Motorway

Once there were swans
Every year they came
To the canal they came
But the boys went and killed them
With bricks and planks of wood
They broke their wings
They battered and stabbed them
With bottles, nails and clubs
They laughed a lot
They thought it was really funny

Watching those white feathers
Turning red
Afternoons and evenings
Turning red

I was afraid
When I passed those boys
I was saddened
If only my tears could have healed their wounds
Their bloody hearts
Then they would have flown

Now the canal has been drained
Of all hope of swans
There is none
No more water to drown in
To claim the hapless child
While his mother hangs the washing
He drinks with the boys
Helping to build a motorway
Where the swans once swam
Turning red
Concrete and steel
Turning red

I am not afraid
When I pass those boys
I am saddened
If only my tears could choke them
Damn their bloody hearts
They will never fly.

Easterhouse, 1977

Sean Clerkin

Whither the Welfare State

Blair's New Labour Government are demonising the poor. Blair, Brown and Co are openly talking about the deserving and undeserving poor which has led to increased usage of terms such as lazy, feckless workshy and scroungers. The Bella magazine found in a survey that one fifth of respondents wanted the male partner in unemployed families to be sterilised. New Labour and their media cronies are creating a climate of fear and hatred.

Within this climate of intolerance Blair is pushing ahead with his great project, the impoverishment of the poor through the dismantling of the Welfare State. In so doing the rich and middle classes will not have to pay their fair share of taxation.

The process of dismantling the Welfare State has begun. Lone parent benefits were cut substantially and even with the Budget supposedly restoring the value of the cuts 60,000 Lone Parents will be worse off by over £2 per week. 9,000 of the most severely disabled people through the operation of the Benefit Integrity Project have had their Disability Allowance cut or stopped. These are people who require a lot of help in their every day lives. Essentially these vulnerable people are having their dignity stolen from them.

In the first six months of the New Labour Government between May and November 1997 326,520 sick and disabled people had their Incapacity Benefit taken off them. This has continued in 1998 with many sick and disabled people losing between £20 and £70 a week. More recently Government Sources leaked to the Times that Incapacity Benefit would be cut to the level of the Job Seekers Allowance.

73,000 unemployed people had their Job Seekers Allowance stopped altogether in the first six months of the New Labour Government. Again this has continued in 1998 with ten of thousands of families being denied Job Seekers Allowance due to people being judged on a subjective basis of not being available for work etc. Therefore families for periods of up to a month have to survive on nothing. The Social

Fund which gives out loans that the poor have to pay back has failed dismally as up to two million people have been denied help they were eligible for because they were deemed as not being able to pay back the loans. This has resulted in the poor falling through the safety net and becoming prey for Loan Sharks etc. falling into the worst form of destitution. The list goes on and on.

Apologists for New Labour state that the Unemployed and Unwaged will be helped back to work through the New Deal. The truth is that the New Deal is just another 'revolving door' scheme where the 'New Dealers' (those between 18 and 25) as they are known will either be put on the employment option at £60 a week, the voluntary sector or environmental task force options at £53.90 a week or the education option at £38.90 a week. At the end of their six months on the New Deal many will be unemployed again as New Labour are not creating any permanent jobs as part of the so-called New Deal.

The Free Market will not create the required number of jobs to reduce unemployment. The OECD has predicted that unemployment will rise by at least 200,000 in Britain in 1999. New Labour's crusade is against inflation and needs a high rate of unemployment as part of this policy to bring inflation down. The Government is intent on driving the long term unemployed, the long term sick and disabled and Lone Parents off Social Security Benefits no matter the human cost.

The other pillars of the Welfare State; Education, The National Health Service, and Public Sector Housing are in the process of being privatised with Private Consortia looking to make a commercial return of 5-6% making these services much more expensive than if they remained in the Public Sector. Council taxes will increase, patient services will decline, and market rents will need to be paid.

It is in this climate of the dismantling of the Welfare State that the National Petition Against Poverty was launched and has been successful so far in that 37,500 people have signed the National Petition. We are calling on the Government to redistribute income and wealth to the poor ensuring that the rich and middle classes pay for the restoration of Full Employment for those that want to work and to increase Social Security Benefit in line with the change in average earnings and not as is currently done, with benefits being increased in line with price inflation.

Unless the above is done Professor David Piachaud's prediction that an extra one to two million people will end up in poverty will happen because of New Labour Government policies. We who are involved in the National Petition Against Poverty will consolidate the gains made by taking the Campaign Against Poverty into every local community empowering all of the poor to fight back together against A New Labour Government hell bent on attacking the poor and vulnerable.

The March and Rally that the NPAP held on 17th March 1998 against Welfare Cuts showed the low paid, the disabled, lone parents, pensioners, the homeless, students and the unemployed making Common Cause in the campaign against Free Market inspired poverty. This marked a turning point where previously sections of the poor have campaigned in isolation from one another e.g. pensioners and lone parents.

We have a lot to learn from the unemployed and homeless in France who have become a real thorn in the side of the French Government through Non Violent Civil Disobedience. It took the poor in France three years to unite sufficiently in Common Cause to force concessions from the French Government.

The National Petition Against Poverty being composed of community activists, the homeless, the disabled, lone parents, pensioners, students and the unemployed also want to make Common Cause with the trade union movement and others in the fight to retain and enhance the Welfare State. The NPAP will challenge the New Labour Government and the Capitalist Establishment at every opportunity to ensure that the issue of poverty is at the top of everyone's political agenda so action will be taken in the form of creating real jobs with real wages and giving those who cannot work a decent income enabling them to live independent lives. Local Communities must be directly involved in managing redistributed resources in relation to sustainable economic development to ensure that the local environment is protected and that local unemployed and unwaged members of these communities access employment opportunities. Community empowerment is about communities controlling the material resources that can transform human lives.

New Labour's propaganda machine will state that these ideas are a pipe dream as Britain is spending £100 billion per year on social Security and therefore the United Kingdom faces a welfare explosion, a 'welfare timebomb'. This is a tissue of lies. Britain spends less on Social Security than any comparable nation, just 13 percent of its Gross Domestic Product. The rich can very much afford to pay for improvements in society.

What is lacking is the political will, the compassion and altruism that is needed to take effective action against poverty. We all need to raise our horizons to visualise a better and more socially just society and bury forever the rampant greed and corruption of Thatcherism which the New Labour Government carries around as a badge of pride.

Farquhar McLay

The Crumrush Story

I am at one end of a bench in George Square. A resting place. Legs crossed at the feet, hands in trouser pockets, head thrown well back, face to the summer sky, eyes shut but not asleep. A can of lager on the bench beside me.

At the other end, wearing a khaki greatcoat, a gentleman in angry discourse with the unseen. Several of the unseen. They have been having a go at him since I came here half-an-hour ago. But he gives back as good as he gets. "Don't fret yir sweet fuckin arses," he growls, "the likes o yous urnae up tae it, no wi me onywye, no wi me. I wis top dog, get it? That's it, try it, son. Even if yi get me yi cannae keep me – I'll spill myself. You'll fuckin see, sonny boy. That erysipelas bastard in the white! That dick head!"

From time to time he swings a punch. Other times he half rises and makes a grab at his tormentors. He would stomp them under his heel if only he could get a grip on them. It looks like they always elude him.

His antics are frightening off the respectable citizenry who come by looking for a sit-down. It is just right for me. I can do without the crush. The space between Khaki and me remains nicely unoccupied except for my lager.

Then these three exhausted-looking Orientals trudge into the scene. They're taking snapshots of the stone equestrians, Victoria and Albert, just above us. They clock the bench and they're slowly wending their weary way over.

I'm praying Khaki will start smiting the air again just about now. But no matter. Help is on hand from quite another source. It's the juggernaut Crumrush bearing down on them from the flank. He overtakes and cuts a swathe through the tourists, a plump girl of refined mien and two scrawny youths, all wearing glasses.

They stand stockstill with their cameras hanging limp and stare at the man bulldozing past with the bulged and battered old suitcase. He is in his usual state of dilapidation, walking sideways, his shirt burst open at the neck and the tie, a stringy affair with minute, tortured knot trailing behind him in the gentle breeze. Set on the back of his head is a white showerproof hat of Italian origin – memento of a holiday in Florence a long while back, when earnings were better. He now raises the hat in greeting. "It is you. I thought it was you. Boots taking his ease."

He puts down the suitcase, gives Khaki an appraising glance, hands me my lager and plumps himself down beside me. He folds his arms and leans towards me.

"Old soldiers' reunion, is it?"

I can see he's kind of pleased with himself about something. It occurs to me he might even be in funds. Nobody can be more generous than Walter when he has a few quid. Not that that is very often, not lately anyway. He's been on a bad streak, that's for sure. But nothing lasts forever. So I'm beginning to let myself think about a rib dinner in the Briggait and maybe a pint, or a couple of pints even, to wash it down. It wouldn't be the first time I've been lucky with Walter. But my hopes take a plunge when he says: "What a morning it's been! You wouldn't credit it. I haven't stopped once. From Maryhill to Shawlands Cross and back. From Byres Road to Yoker to Anniesland to Partick. All over the shop. No breakfast, no bus fares, nothing. I'm just this minute out of Zammara's. What a morning!"

A taxing pilgrimage, even without the suitcase, and even for a younger man than Walter. But he has a strong constitution. As he says himself, the constitution of a plutocrat! That's his background. Gastronomically speaking, an excellent background. He had a good start in life. All that bourgeois feeding in childhood, training him up for power in the boardroom. You can see how it has stood him in good stead. As heir to the Crumrush fortune he had to develop robust appetites. They say it's the first years that count. Now he's as strong as an ox.

"I don't know how you do it, Walter. That case would kill me."

"Ha! That's only half. On good days I have two cases."

Yes I can see how it was. Pampered daily with extravagant delicacies. What feasts they had! Partridges and pheasant and roast goose, of venison that fattest haunch, broiled hams, 12oz steaks with creamy sauce and spinach. Second helpings wheeled in and downed by the basin and the bucketful. Every meal a banquet. When they brought in Walter's food the platters groaned. No one had ever seen such eating. Much petted Walter after the tragedy of his mother's death when he was eleven. She went to the lake and drowned herself. Walter's only comfort was Mirabelle, the chambermaid. She did all she could.

Walter's father liked to have Mirabelle nearby at mealtimes. She assisted in a variety of ways. Frequently she would carve a morsel and wave it teasingly between father and son before dropping it into one or the other's gaping maw to great screeches of merriment all round. She was kept busy wiping their fingers and mouths and tucking in their towels. People were always saying that Walter's father had a 'thing' for Mirabelle.

"So give me your opinion, Boots. Advise me. With two cases like that, would I do better with a car? Most people say I should get myself wheels. 'Look how you torture yourself! Look at the business you must be missing!' But I'll tell you something, you need more than wheels in this job."

Walter takes off his spectacles and wipes them with great deliberation.

"In this job you have to push and keep pushing. It's nothing more than that. O it was easier once, before the whole world went upmarket. But you still had to push. And I'll tell you something else, I know people with cars who get turned away. And they get discouraged. And they get sick. And they run home and fall into bed. And car or no car, that's them done for. Not me. Look at this – no lunch, no bus fares, nothing, I keep going."

Walter is now rolling his head about to loosen up the neck muscles.

"You know me, Boots. I only speak about what I know. Look at that case. That case would kill you, right? It's mostly rug samples. That's the worst there is. But most days, as I say, I have two cases like that, that's if I have some bus-fare. If I had three hands I'd have three cases. You think I love my work? Don't be daft. I don't love my work. I should be on holiday like you. But listen. I have never taken a penny Social Security in my life. The State doesn't know I exist. That's the way I like it. It's a question of principle. Plenty of times I have nothing. You know it for a fact. I eat broken biscuits. I drink black tea. I've done somersaults with hunger up and down these streets. Do I run with my hat in my hand to the Social? I could never do it. A question of principle."

Just then Khaki starts up about how he fucks his enemies – sometimes in the mouth and sometimes in the arsehole. Walter looks from me to Khaki and back again.

"This is good company you're keeping, Boots. You pick up some funny people. Is this man shell-shocked or what? It's the mud of Flanders on that coat, no doubt. Looks like puke to me. Making your day, is he?"

The boy had the appetite of thirty hogs. When Walter was at table the earth shook. Loud roars of approval from his father as dish after dish came under ferocious attack. The results were messy and even terrifying. The servants shrank back, hiding their eyes. Only Mirabelle kept her composure. She would stay till the boy was sated and lead him to the ottoman where he liked to stretch out and be massaged.

Whenever he saw them like that, the recumbent boy, the son and heir on whom he doted, and the selfless Mirabelle ministering to his every need, the manufacturer's being was suffused with a wonderful sense of the rightness of things: that there were indeed some few shards of justice left in a bleak and bedevilled world.

Walter throws his left arm over the back of the bench, and the right leg over the left. He watches his swinging right brogue. He smoothes the grey stubble on his upper lip.

"I went up to Zammara's today. First time. Zammara has a reputation you know. Not a nice man. No manners. No finesse. You don't sell your personality with Zammara. He doesn't give a tinker's turd for your personality – only the goods. He's a bit of an ogre. Hardly ever talks. The best spiel in your repertoire is wasted on him. In fact it only get his back up. All the reps know Zammara. They're terrifed to go near him. I've listened to all the stories. If your stuff is wrong he kicks holes in your suitcase, pushes you out the door, blackballs you for good – sine die. Kaput! Time is money with Zammara. You go away feeling like a worm, and you never get back in. But I have to take a chance. Unpaid bills are piling up – rent, electricity, polltax. My stomach is shrinking. I don't care if he kicks holes in **me**, never mind the suitcase – Zammara is my last hope, kept back for this day, at my lowest ebb. The one unturned stone."

"Jesus!" I say, putting the can to my mouth, "as bad as that?"

"Well, you know me, Boots. You know my history. I've seen a bit of life, the good and the bad. And I've been many things in my time but never a coward. I've braved worse bastards than Zammara and never flinched. And even if I am starving, at least I know it's not because fear got the better of me. It's not because I backed down."

"You did right. Walter. What's a few kicks if you get peace of mind?"

It was plain that the widow-man Crumrush had taken a fancy to Mirabelle. He liked to follow her about the house and watch as she performed her various chores. He liked it best when she rolled up her sleeves – the movements of her bare, deliciously rounded arms fascinated and delighted him in ways which, at first, he could hardly fathom. But then came that bright morning in early spring when Mirabelle went out to beat carpets beneath the master's window.

As he watched, the fading dynast became transfixed in all his senses – a sudden mysterious kindling of joyful tremors coursed through him, and the longer he watched, the more his passion grew, till he was utterly overcome by an insane craving which nothing could check.

It was a fateful day for the House of Crumrush. Later they questioned whether the chambermaid was entirely innocent of the effect her vigorous charms had on middle-aged gentlemen of the better classes.

It was a question never satisfactorily resolved. Certainly the little notes slipped beneath her door in the night – little notes lovingly composed and bordering on fairly explicit, not to say crude, intentionality – could ultimately have left her in no doubt as to the precise nature of the master's perverted longings.

"So I breeze in," says Walter. "A cheery smile for all and sundry. Mr. Happy at your service! The whole emporium turns and stares. This young lad with a trolley offers to help. A tall, shapely lady dressed all in black is pointed out to me. A Miss Frick, Mr Zammara's personal assistant. She is over by the elevators. She is going through some important-looking documents. She has a deeply disdainful look on her face. I stride towards her. "Miss Frick, isn't it? Good morning, how are you?' She looks me up and down. She stares at the suitcase. 'I'm sorry,' she says, 'Mr Zammara is not available.'

"She presses angrily at the button on the wall. The lift comes. We both get in. 'What a pity!' I say. 'I was so looking forward to seeing him. I have some new lines I know would interest him.' She stays cold and aloof. She finds it easy to disbelieve people. The lift stops at the third floor. She gets out. I get out. 'It's not his day for seeing reps,' she says. 'Come in next Monday.'

"She sets a brisk pace through Household Furniture with me losing ground on the outside. 'O dear, I shall be in Manchester all day Monday, I'm afraid. Won't be back in this neck of the woods for another month at least. And I did promise to look in with these new things.'

"She stops to parley with a young salesman. He's at his desk writing a receipt. She keeps me in the corner of her eye. I pretend to be interested in the workmanship of a cocktail cabinet – a paltry bit of junk like everything else in his damned emporium. Then she makes a sudden dash for the carpet department, but I'm soon up close once again and going good. Members of staff are giving us funny looks.

"I keep yapping on about new lines not to be missed. Disdain is cracking. Irritation is setting in. Now we're back at the lifts. We're zooming to the basement. 'Perhaps I could leave some samples in the care of your good self – of course they're rather bulky." We are thundering through Hardware & Electrical. 'This is hardly a suitable time,' she says. But I sense she's weakening. I'm destroying her usual effect on the underlings.

"We move into Wallpapers & Paint, neck and neck. I'm stumbling and staggering at her elbow, doing a kind of kangaroo hop at tricky

94

corners. I'm just about knackered. It can't last. Something has to give. We hear a titter. That's it! That's it! That's what I was waiting for. She stops. Her mouth falls open. She's disgusted and breathless at the same time. She closes her eyes and waves me away from her. 'All right,' she says, 'all right. Don't move from here. I'll send someone.'

" 'I'll be here, don't worry,' I say. 'I'm in no rush.' She gives me a long pained look and away she goes, much relieved I'm not following. But wait. The man she sends – my God I nearly fell down with the shock – it's McCafferty. My old friend McCafferty. You've heard me on about McCafferty. My next-door neighbour in West Princes Street. Cecil Ignatius McCafferty, M.A., formerly of University College, Dublin – pedagogue and child-molester. I used to visit him in Barlinnie. What a stroke of luck!"

Mirabelle, however, was not all that taken with Crumrush the Elder – "that sweaty old goat with the dribbly snout!" as she was wont to characterise him in private. Certainly Walter's father, County Councillor and JP, had more to him, in the way of blemish no less than adornment, than simply the nose on his face. But not for Mirabelle. For Mirabelle the master **was** *his nose – bulbous and pock-marked and with little clumps of ginger hair sprouting out of it. All of which, let it be said, the easy-going Mirabelle might have pardoned as venial: but the pendulous bead of water at the tip stirred in her a wave of revulsion which no amount of amiability could have withstood.*

Not even the direful prospect of losing her position at the hall, nor even of going to jail at the next assizes, could have induced her to answer the night-time summons to the master's chamber. As a consequence the chore invariably passed to the obliging Mrs Goldie, the butler's wife, who acted as housekeeper. She was a diminutive lady of quite startling obesity. Her ungainly form was kept shrouded in a massive hooded cloak which she wore day and night, indoors and out.

Many a night Mirabelle listened for the swoosh of that cloak in the passage as the housekeeper, in a laboured little trot, made what haste she could in the direction of the master.

"So you scored?" I say, my hopes again taking wing.

"Well, maybe. Time will tell. I mean McCafferty's devious. But just look at this," he adds, taking out a notebook and turning the pages. "The biggest order I've had this year. A commission, I'd say, somewhere in the region of three hundred quid."

"Come on, rat face!" Khaki says.

"The thing is," Walter goes on, "Zammara has to approve it. If McCafferty plays straight we're ok. I think it scared him a wee bit, me turning up like that. I mean, the things I know about the man. One careless word overheard in that place and he's out. He knows that. O he'll do his best to wangle it through. I have faith in McCafferty."

It was quite different with the son, though. For it was the bewitching Mirabelle, one hot June day with nobody about, who rescued young Walter from his obsessive devotion to food, and lifted him clean out of his terrible torpor. She admitted him to a world of delights beside which all other pastimes seemed as dull as oatmeal. She roused in him a hunger for her flesh which stilled all former hungerings. They indulged each other's needs as frequently as opportunity permitted. In the night-time their noisy dalliance often reached the ears of the fat dwarf as she swooshed past the chambermaid's door en route for the master.

"When will they pay you?" I ask, fearing the worst.

"O not for months. But the main thing is this: all going well, I now have a foot in the door. They're only easy dealing with the people they deal with. That's the secret. Thanks to McCafferty I am now one of that small select band."

"Fine. But what do you do meantime?"

"I make more calls."

However, one day, apprised by the lickspittle butler (set on by the awful Mrs Goldie) that Mirabelle had tempted and corrupted the young master, and ignited in the boy dark lusts which she gleefully and with expert usage gratified nightly in her chamber and sometimes in the rushes by the lake on Saturday Afternoons – Crumrush senior was stricken to the marrow of his balls, and, with low oaths and scurrilous abuse, he vengefully, and in a furious rage, dismissed the chambermaid and had her booted out of the stately mansion, leaving to love-lorn Walter, who now had one appetite too many, long nights of inconsolable grief as he pined for his lost Mirabelle.

I offer Walter the remains of the lager. He refuses with a quick little shake of the head, giving me a rather pitying look.

"Never on an empty stomach," he says, pulling the white hat down over his eyes.

Mirabelle's successor, a frosty Rechabite of mature years, thoroughly vetted and approved by Mrs Goldie, was quickly found. As for Walter, it was decided that he should accompany some Crumrush & Co Sales Executives to Hamburg for a Trade Fair. It would last three weeks.

In Hamburg he would extend his acquaintance in the business world, pick up invaluable selling experience, improve his German, and at a judiciously selected brothel rid himself of his stupid infatuation for the slut Mirabelle. It was, in large measure, Mrs Goldie's plan, evidence of the ascendancy which the butler's wife had now gained over Walter's father, for it was no secret, such was his overwhelming concern for his son's good, that old Crumrush could not bear to be parted from the boy, not even for a single day.

"Too bad you didn't hit him for a fiver when you were at it," I put in snidely, "just to tide you over, like."

Walter titters dryly.

"Just to make an arse of the whole thing, you mean."

Yes Walter was pining. All appetite for cooked meat had gone. He had grown lean and wan and solitary. He took to wandering aimlessly, or so it seemed, about the estate and beyond. He was not infrequently to be found loitering on the bleak hillside, a wild look in his eye, uttering a weird kind of moan which made the sheep scamper off in alarm.

"But isn't that just typical?" Walter is saying. "The man throws me a lifeline, and all you can think about is why I didn't try wheedling a fiver out of him. I don't know why I talk to you."

Mirabelle, on the other hand, did not pine. Even had she been of a pining disposition, which she certainly was not, cold and hunger would pretty soon have jerked her out of it. As a first necessity she had to find employment. But where? With her good name fatally besmirched – the Crumrush household had seen to it that every kind of evil was laid on her – the gentry spurned her as a domestic, which was the only work she knew. Wherever she applied the door was slammed in her face.

"You'd think I was blackmailing him or something."
"Well…"
"It was business! Just business! You find that hard to understand, I know. That's your wino mentality coming out. If I thought like that I'd be in the gutter like you and the loony here."

Sylvester McEntee, however, the proprietor of the Coach and Four, was not a man to be swayed by malicious tittle-tattle. If it put pound notes in his till, he found he could overcome the common prejudices of the county without too much difficulty. At the first sight of Mirabelle he knew he'd struck gold. "What we need in this howff," he had often mused, totting up the meagre take after a long day, and thinking betimes of his dear wife's now flattened posteriors, "is a woman with a good bum!" And Mirabelle's was of a splendour and magnitude the equal of which he had not rested a hand on in many a year.

She was, thought Sylvester, the type of joyous woman who would of a certainty draw custom. She was out-going and zestful and with a mischievous eye to delight and beguile any drinker. He also knew he would get her cheap, a lass in her shoes being in no position to haggle over wages. She did not haggle, and got the job.

"Maybe you'd like that, ey? Shall I join the odds and sods, the jakies and junkies, the shipwrecked and unlovely trashcan brigade? Tell me, Boots, would you like that? Me in the mire with you and your Khaki friend. Me with my helpful little fiver, and you half-sloshed and him as crazed as a cuckoo – sunk in shit, beyond hope, the three of us. Wouldn't that be nice and cosy!"

It was the reptile butler, Mr Goldie, who spied her there one night, about a week later, serving drinks in the snug, laughing and joking and clearly a great favourite with the whole clientele – some high nobs among them, men of business and gentlemen farmers. Word quickly got to Crumrush and put him in a panic. For him, Mirabelle had been as good as dead. He was suddenly reminded of the thousand-and-one shit-smeared billets-doux he'd pushed under her door. What if they were still in her possession?

And what stories might she not spread regarding other singularities of his household, such as the nocturnal jaunts of Mrs Goldie? In the Coach and Four Mirabelle would have an eager audience. His standing in the county would plummet. The respected burgher would bite the dust. For a week he waited in torment for the blackmail attempt which the chambermaid was surely planning. He took £5 from the safe in his study and that night, dejected and tearful, confided in the fat dwarf.

"Well, I'm sorry, gentlemen," Walter chuckles, "I'm really very sorry, but I cannot oblige. I am not cut out for it. It so happens I have work to do. Yes, WORK!"

Mrs Goldie sternly reproved the master. What a simpleton he was! He must on no account pay her a penny piece. And anyway, it would never come to blackmail. That soft fool Mirabelle didn't have it in her. She would be too busy getting humped.

It was his nerves getting the better of him. She pointed out that he was magistrate as well as a manufacturer. And a certain establishment's drinks license might easily be placed under threat. Crumrush was quick to get her drift. No publican would risk his licence for a barmaid. And for Mirabelle, after the Coach and Four, there would now quite definitely be nothing left. She would have to flee the county to find work. How simple it all was. How glad he was a magistrate! The House of Commons was not beyond him yet. He would set the necessary wheels in motion at once. The publican would be easy meat.

"Fuck-bags, the lot o yi!" Khaki yells.
He turns to Walter.
"I fuckin know this place. I know where we ur aaright. Dae you?"
Walter nods and quickly looks away.

But before letting her go, the proprietor of the Coach and Four made plain to Mirabelle the pressures that had been put on him, and by whom, and advised her that, if she ever meant to prosper, she had better keep well out of range of that evil bastard in the big house. Mirabelle thanked him, and said that such indeed was her plan. And so it was, but not quite her whole plan.

"Fuckin chanty-wrasslers, the lot o yi!" Khaki says, as he cranes forward and twists himself round til he's staring straight up Walter's nose.

Walter nods solemnly. "I know how you feel."

Over Khaki's hunched shoulders I watch the Jap girl posing for a snapshot between the lions at the cenotaph. Definitely one for the Tokyo album.

Walter is edging away from the crusted vomit on Khaki's coat.

Khaki twirls a finger in the air. "This place!" he growls, "this place! Dae you know where we ur?"

Walter looks about him with comic exaggeration.

"This place?" says Walter. "Why, if I mistake not, this is the Merchant City – reborn!"

"Naw, this," says Khaki, in a sing-song, whinnying snarl, "**this is the fuckin balmy cane!**"

Mirabelle bade farewell to the publican McEntee, took up her suitcase and stepped across the street to the railway station where she consulted the irascible station-master, Sloan, from whom she enquired the times of trains going to the city. Sloan, the last remaining member of a tiny religious sect which had failed to take root in the county, was a recluse. A long, lean individual, he had a fairly low opinion of human beings in general, and a particular contempt for human beings who couldn't read time-tables. All he asked was to be left in peace to cultivate cabbages in his nearby allotment. If he had on occasion to wave a flag and blow a whistle, well, so be it, that was his cross in life, and it paid his wages. He wasn't paid to be polite and he didn't care if the whole world knew it.

So judge of Mirabelle's surprise when she found this old sour-puss, the disobliging Sloan, bubbling over with generous impulses. He invited her up to his living-quarters, a comfy little parlour above the ticket office, his "den" as he called it, where he kept the master timetable, or so he said. He supplied her with all the information she needed and stacks that she didn't. He offered her tea and some buttered scones, home-baked, he assured her, after his mother's recipe; his only weakness. He showed her a faded photograph of his mother, a lady of resolute countenance, seated with the Good Book spread open before her, and staring, with more than a hint of repugnance, Mirabelle thought, at the small boy standing at her knee – a sprightly aspirant with more scamp then seraph looking out of him. His poor mother was now with the Lord. Then he played a few records on his wind-up gramophone – Gospel songs about a good time not far off. He knew all the songs by heart, and shouted out every other line before the tenor got to sing it. He made frantic signals to Mirabelle to join in, which she did, feeling very foolish, and Sloan clapped his hands with delight.

After a while Mirabelle had to interrupt these proceedings and ask if he would be kind enough to look after her suitcase while she transacted some urgent business in the village. He said it was against regulations for the station-master to take in luggage as the railway accepted no responsibility for loss or damage; but, as a special favour to her, he would be glad to make an exception and was, in fact, only too happy to be of service no matter what. Then with a lewd smirk he added that he had a pretty good idea what her urgent business would be. Mirabelle smiled and ate the scone and drank the tea as Sloan, kneeling by her chair, put his hand up her skirt. Mirabelle said it was, unfortunately, business that could not wait and had to be attended to immediately, but when she returned, if there was time, she might be able to relieve him, by one means or another, of his heavy burden, and he should not lose heart.

"I know, I know," Walter says. "It's a point of view. Balmy it might well be. But I for one would rather be up the pole than down the stank!"

On the six-mile bus ride out to the Crumrush estate Mirabelle's mood surprised her. She had anticipated tremors and palpitations in the course of this journey, and blind panic when she came in sight of the lodge gates. Now it was happening for real, her mood was easy, even buoyant. She could smile at the thought of Mr Sloan: seeing him like the boy in the picture, hungry for his mother's buttered scones; and hungry still. And yet the episode at the railway station had hurt her deeply. If her ill repute had reached as far as the hermit Sloan, it was indeed time she was out of it.

They wanted her out and she would go. But they would have to pay a price. Her heart leapt at the thought. Poor Mirabelle capable of exacting a price! It was a feeling she could get to like.

The hour was strange to Mirabelle. It was unusual for her to be out and about in the middle of the day. The big world with its busy people and their homely doings all semmed to Mirabelle, at that strange hour, to be only very faintly familiar, only faintly human, even. Of course she knew these people. They were neighbours, a safe and couthie lot. She knew all about them, where they were going to and coming from, and who was doing what to whom. Just for a moment it was like the clockwork peep-show she'd seen as a child. The same dreary scene over and over till your pennies ran out. All these serious people going here and there, and back and forth, the strutting gallants, the angelic girls, and near them the drab pensioners queuing, smiling, like in a safe and happy dream. She had fallen from that sleepy world.

So not bothering to look any more. Detached now, and glad to be so, as the bus raced on. Journeying now with the scent of Crumrush in her nostrils, and that nice feeling rising up again – the feeling she could get to like, glad to have found it.

"Just think back to what we were," says Walter. "Nothing but a crumbling, shitty little cesspit. A malignancy. A smelly, ugly rat-hole of the defeated and debased. This smiling face, even if it is a bit half-witted, is surely an improvement.

Mirabelle made her way into the Crumrush estate through adjoining woodland which, at the rear of the house, came up almost to the gardens. She noted the small blue motor car parked in the main driveway – Mr Mallet's, young Walter's tutor. She moved round further to the rear of the turreted mansion and close enough, though still in the shelter of the trees, to have a perfect view of the window as well as the doorway that led to the servants' staircase. As dusk approached, and lights were switched on and off in various rooms, Mirabelle, knowing the run of the house, could plot the whereabouts of the occupants with a fair degree of exactitude.

The master had moved out of his study and into the bedroom, then returned to the study for a moment or two before re-entering the bedroom where he would rest before dinner. Walter would be in the library with Mallet. The butler and Mrs Goldie had come downstairs.

They would be having their early-evening break, sipping the master's Madeira and trading stories about the "wrong 'uns" they'd had to deal with in their time. Having each spent a lifetime in service, ever abject and ever vigilant, they had wide experience of "wrong 'uns".

The thought made Mirabelle smile. She knew the kind of mauling they would subject her to, the venom they'd expend on her till she was mush. All their stories ended the same way. Getting kicked out was the end of "wrong 'uns", they never came back.

She had her eyes on Walter's window, still in darkness, when the door opened and Mallet stepped out, a bald little man with his hat in his hand. He looked right and left, and up and down, then turned about and, to Mirabelle's astonishment, peed copiously up against the manor wall. After that he moved slowly up the gravel path to the drive where his little blue car awaited him.

Just as Mallet drove away, the light went on in Walter's room, and Mirabelle slipped quickly through the garden and entered the house. She could hear voices in the pantry below as they prepared the evening banquet. Treading warily on the creaking steps, she mounted the staircase to the second floor. She reached Walter's door without mishap, turned the handle and went in.

"Or at least an improvement from my point of view," says Walter, a friendly hand on Khaki's shoulder to hold him off. "I speak, you understand, not as a native of the place, although I've been here, on and off, for close to forty years. Unlike your good self I had no early inurement in squalor and degradation. It was a hard slog for me to acclimatise myself. I was born to something quite different."

It was now, only now, in the fevered embrace of her young lover, that Mirabelle might have faltered. The boy was consumed with joy. He clung to her. He wept. He babbled. He twined her hair round his fingers. He poked the dimples in her cheeks. He was entirely hers, to do with as she liked, which was exactly as she knew it would be and suited her purpose perfectly. At the same time, his utter helplessness made her uneasy. She could see he was afraid of her and what she could do to him. Having lost her once, he was terrified of it ever happening again, and at odd moments, as Mirabelle was quick to notice, his face clouded over with dread.

The boy quivered as she nestled him. She might have faltered. Far from exacting a price, she could, for all she knew, be paying one, and a very heavy one, in linking her fate to Walter's. But she had come too far to back off now.

"For me," says Walter, "a slum was just stench and putrefaction. For you, it was home and kindergarten. I quite see why you miss it. Personally, these streets used to terrify me, just as now, with all these new changes, all this high-class living, they obviously terrify you. But I have good news for you, my friend. You'll get used to it. You'll even get to love it. Yes, love it!"

Mirabelle threw open the doors of a cupboard, rummaged about and came out with a small canvas hold-all. She looked at Walter. He might easily be a handsome enough man in a year or two, once he got free of this place.

He would be strong too, she could see that, once he got some real work to do. Why not? In the village she'd seen quarrymen not half Walter's size. In a year or two there would be no stopping him. The thought eased her mind.

They sat on the bed together and Mirabelle said he must pay close attention to what she had to say. In a few minutes they were going away together, far away, and would not be parted again, but to do that, and to do it right, they needed money, quite a lot of money, and she knew, and he knew, that in his father's study there was a safe, and in the safe was a whole heap of money, and if Walter could get hold of the key to the safe, which she knew, and he knew, his father kept about him on his person, in one or other of his pockets, Walter could fill this – the hold-all – with all the money in the safe and fetch it back here to Mirabelle, without his father or anybody else being any the wiser, and

104

they would be off together in a trice! She handed him the hold-all,
opened the door and pushed him out.
Five minutes later he returned, all smiles, the hold-all well weighted.
"Did you remember to close the safe?" asked Mirabelle. Walter
nodded. "And return the key?" Walter looked hurt. "I did everything
– just the way you said." She took him by the hand. They made their
way downstairs unseen, unheard. They went out through the woods,
the way Mirabelle had come. Before the bus arrived, Mirabelle
handed Walter some change for his fare, and on boarding they took
separate seats, as arranged, with Mirabelle in charge of the bag.
At the railway station, Sloan looked sick with disappointment when
he saw her with Walter in tow. But catching something in Mirabelle's
glance, his hopes revived, and all three quickly repaired to Sloan's
"den" upstairs.
In the hour or so before their train was due, Walter sipped some tea
and munched a couple of buttered scones and played records on the
gramophone, and Mirabelle relieved Sloan, two or three times, of his
heavy burden – thus, she hoped, and she wasn't wrong, ensuring his
silence should any inquiries be made concerning his two guests in the
days that followed.
And Mirabelle and Walter got clean away.

"You'll see, you'll see," shouts Walter. "However badly it treats you,
one day you'll cease to notice. One day, quite suddenly, you'll feel at
home. It's only my adopted city, remember – adopted, I may say,
rather more from necessity than choice – but I got used to it, I got to
love it, yes even the old slums, even the rat- and bug-ridden tenement,
even the single-end with the stairhead loo, and the TB and the rickets
and the scabies, and Dixon's Blazes belching out its filth, and all those
tiny white coffins one used to see. O yes, I got used to it. I soon got
into the swing of things. It'll be the same for you. It's only a matter of
time. If it doesn't kill you first, that is. You have to make sure it
doesn't kill you first. That above all."
Khaki recoils sharply. "Kill **me**?"
Walter tried to backtrack. "No, no, what I mean is… "
Khaki gets to his feet, looks about him anxiously, takes a few paces
up and down, and comes back and stands over us, his head inclined

heavily to one side. He is swinging his arms up and down from the elbow. "Kill **me**?"

"You could be a waiter," Walter puts in quickly. "Do you know that? They can make anybody into a waiter. It's the coming thing, I'll tell you. Yes, mark my words, with all these tourists and everything this town will very soon need all the waiters it can get. So don't be so depressed. Pick yourself up, man. I can see a time coming when we'll all be waiters. Get yourself a tie. They can make anybody into a waiter, believe me. I was in catering once myself –" he turns to me – "did I ever tell you?"

"I'll eat the bastards!" says Khaki, stomping away from us. "I'll fuckin eat them!"

"Sure I was," Walter runs on, "that other time when things were bad. No work anywhere. I was in the Beresford. Now that was an hotel, boy! The best in Glasgow. It was classy. I was in the kitchen. Assistant cook, would you believe? Put on two stone inside a month, and half of Glasgow dying of malnutrition! Of course they didn't take on just anybody, no, no. Someone had to speak for you. Even a kitchen porter needed three references. But I was all right. My dear late wife worked there many, many years. A well-respected lady. One word from her and…"

Khaki is slouching in the middle of the Square, going this way, then that. People are making long detours to avoid him. He is growling, baring his teeth. From the pavement a young cop has noticed him. The cop, in shirt sleeves, is coming up behind him at a very leisurely pace.

Suddenly Khaki stiffens, looks up, jerks his shoulders back and marches purposefully out of the square.

"Your friend's gone," says Walter, fanning himself with his hat. "He sobered up pretty quick."

He wipes his face and neck and replaces the hat at a sensible angle. "By jeez, it's hot, ey?"

He takes a grip on his suitcase. The three Jap tourists come over and squeeze onto the bench. Walter stands up and takes a deep inhalation of air.

"That's nice. That's a nice breeze."

People in dark glasses are going past. They wear Hawaiian shirts and Bermuda shorts. They have white training shoes on their feet.

I close my eyes again, turning my face to the summer sky. There should be palm trees, one imagines.

Donald Anderson

Educashun! Educashun! Educashun!

Whit a stinker of a topic, for someone who has taken early retirement from teaching, to be asked to contribute to the latest Workless Country forum. At last, after escaping from the chalk face, it's time for others to continue the class war against the weans and leave me in peace tae fight the class war agin their parents in Her Majesty's Loyal, Royal, Imperial Labour Party, who are determined to destroy the traditional Scottish working class respect for free, public education.

As someone who left school at 15 to enter Yoonie in his thirties it was easy to see through the toytown revolutionary student leaders. One did not need crystal balls to predict that they would grow up to be full time Labour careerists sticking it to the working class. My years of heid banging as a shop steward, where I learnt that the workers had to spend more time fighting the bosses' full time, well-heeled, mouthpieces in the Tame Unions than their bosses themselves, taught me that at least.

My last factory job culminated in a six week strike where the workers were chucked out on the stones and the factory removed, lock, stock and barrel, with full Union enthusiastic co-operation, to England. I challenge any British Nationalist, sorry "Inter"nationalist "leftie" to quote me one instance where the Union, Labour Hacks, trendy middle class "Revolutionary" this or "Workers" that groupies, or English factory workers have ever demanded that the work, contracts, machinery, plant, etc, should be blacked and prevented from being moved out of the country (Scotland). Did they ever support demands for parity of wages and conditions for the Scottish workers in the same public and private industries and services?

During the six week strike at Pilkington's Fibreglass factory there was no shortage of trendy Sloan Rangers selling their "revolutionary" papers outside the Pilkington gates of poor Possilpark, now more famous for its "Possil Sweeties" (Temazepam) than its poorly paid former industries, all moved South. Sure it's all the fault of capitalism and not English Nationalism, say the Brits. Tell that to the poor of Possil who are now suffering all the predictable social problems of the transfer of industry and jobs tae the Faitherland. Pilkingtons took over Barr and Stroud at Anniesland where they again employed English management, English foremen and chargehands and the Union paid loyal subservience. When Pilkington was taken over by a French firm the much pretended "Inter"nationalism went oot the windae and the usual anti "frog" racism and jingoism went unheeded by the Union and the trendy GB lefties.

No, I certainly was not impressed by their student wing when I ended up at Strathclyde Yoonie as a mat stud. Nor was I surprised at the venom and black propaganda from their trendy political societies, which were more anti-Scottish in effect than the official Conservative and Unionist Clubs. At least you didn't get any hypocritical, convoluted arguments from them and they admitted that they were Brit Nats without any circuitous arguments. My worst "crime" was to be a founder member of the yoonie 'Scottish Republican Socialist Club' and the yoonie 'John MacLean Society'. John MacLean was a fine chap as an internationalist but of course, totally "insane", when he came out for a Scottish Workers Republic and demanded a Scottish Communist Party. That is not how they would put it, but just engage any in conversation and that would soon become apparent. Just what are the terrors of shoartbreid, 'aggis, tartan, bag-pipes, kilts and Gaelic that substitute for a political debate on Scotland. No TV/Radio discussion or article on Scotland was complete without these instant pundits. If their phobias agin confectionery tins, multi coloured cloths, musical instruments and non-English language were extended to saris, dotis or turbans and Urdu they would rightly be exposed for the racists they are.

The Great British left still repeat this type of nonsense through their London organs to this day and they still love to rewrite Scottish history in silly little pamphlets that would do credit to any BNP literature on the same topic... As their evidence of MacLean's "insanity" they cite the Special Branch reports and two prison screws, sorry doctors. Some revolutionaries eh. Why do they selectively ignore the evidence from Basil Thompson, head of the English

Intelligence, who is on record as saying that he would smear John MacLean and Sylvia Pankhurst by spreading the rumour that they were both mad. The very British "left" also ignore the fact that Sylvia Pankhurst supported John MacLean in his election campaign as a candidate for a Scottish Workers Republic. Why did Lenin and the Bolsheviks make this "madman" the Soviet Consul in Scotland? When MacLean accused the original Communist Party of Great Britain of being a ragbag of opportunists, spies and non - Marxists why do the Brit left ignore the records now naming the spies and the non - Marxist behaviour of many of the leaders who survived on Moscow and London gold? Why do they still accuse MacLean of Paranoia against the evidence of those who were paid to spy on him round the clock? Why do the English Trot Nats resort to Stalin style character assassination of anyone who supports MacLean's policies to this day?

Come to think of it? What happened to all those trendy student Trots of the seventies, who became full time Labourites, Mother of Parliament Members and Tame Union officials, just as I knew they would? Some even fled to the Bahamas as Thatcherite tax exiles. I ended up teaching History and Modern Studies, something I couldn't do now if I had to pay a Labour Loan Shark, Labour Tuition Fees, to be taught English Nationalist History and Politics in Anglicised Universities and Colleges in Scotland. Not with a wife and two weans to keep as a mature student, then go in to debt to pay aff the Labour Loan, no thanks Tony. There were plenty of the Jim Murphy type student leaders who loved to chant, "Tories Out" at student demos and screw the student workers when they were elected to Tory wards like Eastwood to out Thatcher the old Thatcherites. Then it was "Heath Out" (and Lord Wilson in). Very revolutionary eh? I could name the grown up "left" students who froze the workers wages and closed educational establishments and did very well from their careers in the Great British State. But I guess I must be a failure, as they labelled MacLean, Burns and Wallace. Then who wants to be a "successful" class traitor, despite the wages?

Today, Glasgow Cooncil's "left" radical leader is not only closing schools at an alarming rate and leaving whole working class areas denuded, he is also planning to sell them off to the private sector, like cooncil hooses and other slum buildings. The old Progressives built more public services; municipalised the City's water, gas, electricity, transport, schools, public parks, toilets, bandstands, fountains, wells, benches, old men's huts, libraries, public health and public housing, such as Knightswood, etc. Labour built the Drumchapels, etc, closed parks, libraries and couldn't even run public toilets. Is this the Great British Revolution my trendy student chums strived for?

When John asked me to write this article on educashun, I telt him that perhaps I was not the best person, that the schools I taught in were all closed. I taught in John Street, Bridgeton, Greenwood, Castlemilk, Westwood, Easterhouse, Woodside and North Kelvinside. All closed, except the last two which are being run down for closure. Was it something I said? Then I had previously worked in Singers, Royal Ordinance Factory, Fibreglass Ltd and a Co-op factory which closed. I did my National Service in the Cameronians – closed – and served in the Merchant Navy – almost closed. I once joined the IMG (International Marxist Group) which closed to allow its revolutionary members to become Labour MPs and Cooncillors. Maybe I should join HM Labour Party, they're fond o' closures.

Donnie Munro gave up teaching for singing and dancing, then to become an Auld Labour Numptie, tame Tuechter turned Hey Jimmy and New Labour paid apologist for the Glesga New Labourite 'Evening Times'. New Labour also rewarded the 'Evening Times', 'Herald' and STV boss for keeping the Scots public ignorant with a made up job. "Red" Clydesider, Lord Coocaddens, Gus (Call me Ramsay) MacDonald gave up the 'Gorbals Young Socialists' to become an "Inter"national Socialist (English National "Socialist" Workers Party then) and gave that up to become a Labourite again. In line with most other Brit left groups it was SWP policy to 'Vote Labour' and 'Keep Scotland British'. He made sure STV never became a 'Scottish' Television anything, made £5 million by paying off 500 workers, which qualified him for the job of Labour's unelected Minister of Unemployment. Then he recruited JB Sports Owner, Tom Hunter, who sold 500 jobs to England, to his Jobless Creation team, saying that Scotland needed another 100 like him. That would work out at another 500,000 job losses. Whit has Labour goat against Scotland? Ex SWPer, Lord Gus, a self confessed admirer of Thatcher, said he was comfortable with "New" Labour. Tory Blair and Helen (Bobby's Girl) Liddell are also Thatcher admirers.

Blair attended Fettes School in Edinburgh, which is in effect an English private school and has nothing to do with the Scottish education system. What hope for Scottish education now.

At the turn of the century it could understandably be argued that the Catholic Education Act was Liberal or progressive. Now it is understandable that Muslims desire a secular school in Bellahouston. No one can argue against this if these sections of our communities feel threatened. When James Connolly was asked by the Brit "left" (who no more understood Ireland than they do their Scottish Colony) why he supported separate Catholic Schools in Ireland, he replied that, all he knew was that the Catholic Schools produced rebels and the Protestant Schools produced Unionists. Here in Scotland, where he learned his socialist education, we do not have Protestant schools as such, but non-denominational schools, which are now becoming more "mixed", because of mixed marriages and the breakdown of society, etc. I personally think it is time to end all secular schools from a socialist point of view, and from an educational and economical point of view. If we must have religious education then it can be time-tabled as part of the curriculum, along with other subjects, and each pupil can attend the religious education of their choice. This works quite well in other parts of Scotland, especially the rural areas and in England where they are not daft enough to encourage such divisions. Though this can only come from the Catholic population when they are ready and cannot be enforced. Cherlie Marx once said that football was the opium of religion in Glesga. The Old Firm is now a great source of class division and also recruitment for London based groupies. The London based BNP tries to recruit at Ibrox. The London based left like to form psuedo "Irish" fronts and try to recruit at Parheid. Having an "Irish" Freedom Movement based in London is akin to the PLO having its HQ in Tel Aviv. All these fronts' groupies support the British State. All are anti-Scottish (unlike genuine Irish Nationalist groups who do not support the 'Forces of the Crown' against Scotland). All these fronts have a history of State infiltration and direction.

When Ms Remington was appointed head of MI5 she stated quite blatantly in her maiden speech that British Intelligence infiltrated and controlled the Brit left groups, even to the point of running their rallies and deciding their routes. Even if she was lying there would be no need to run the Brit left in Scotland as they seem to have an Imperialistic, British Nationalist, anti-Scottish life of their own. Their infantile student name calling of Scottish Nationalists and Republicans has carried on to their grown-up career days. "Fascist", "Racist", "Na Na Na, Na na". What a perfect royal revolutionary bunch.

Lest anyone accuse me of religious sectarian bias, for daring to propose interdenominational schooling in Scotland, I was raised in Firhill Road, a Jags fan. My parents were a typical Glesga, Heilan-Irish mixed marriage. My brothers and sisters went to different denominational and non-denominational schools together. I became an atheist at the early age of eight when I fun' oot that God was an Englishman.

When Caesar was informed of the plebs rioting in his Imperial City he was asked by his generals if they should bring grain from Egypt or sand for the arenas. "Are you mad", he said. "Bring me sand", and 'Circuses Before Breid' has been Glasgow's misfortune ever since.

John MacLean, who wrote 'Ireland's Tragedy: Scotland's Disgrace' chastised Irish voters at a meeting in the Dixon Halls for singing 'A National Once Again' then voting for the Labour candidate. He told them that if they had voted for him he would not have taken the London train to oppress them, but would have stayed in the Gorbals to defend them and Scottish and Irish freedom. What would he make of the millennium approaching and seeing the City's working class population still sucked into false consciousness and mass idiocy, while the 'Old Firm' directors, and those who stand to gain , get richer and richer while the growing underclass gets poorer and poorer.

Little wonder that John MacLean put so much value on socialist education. His 'Plea for a Scottish Labour College' helped to form thousands of socialists throughout Clydeside. The Labourite 'Workers Education association' is a result of the Labour take over on that front. Another factor explaining the mass socialism of the Scottish Industrial workers of his time compared to the more reactionary workers South of the border was also related to the ability of Scottish workers to read and write, and study classical socialism. The English working class was denied public free education because of religious Anglican secular disputes till the late 1870's and by the First World War Period, unlike the Scottish Workers who owed their literacy advance to the Scottish Reformation.

England did not have a Reformation in the European sense and was more a response to Henry VIII's sexual appetites. His and Elizabeth's military and financial support for Scottish Presbyterianism was more of a political nature as shown by the later Bishops' Wars when the Scots tried to resist English imposition again. Tribal Scotland and Ireland were not part of the deferential English manorial system, dating from the Norman Conquest which subsequent English regimes tried to impose on Scotland, Ireland and Wales. Ireland was not allowed to educate its poorer masses. Trinity College in Dublin and the like was for the benefit of the Anglican ruling class only. Presbyterians were persecuted along with the Catholic majority as witnessed by the mainly Presbyterian United Irishmen. The Orange Order still managed to exclude them till the 1840's, though how they managed to win them over by petty privileges is another story.

Ireland may not have full economic and political freedom yet, but they do have a lot of cultural freedom that the Scots have yet to attain. Irish education has now surpassed that of Scotland, which is also reflecting its run down economy, and thus social problems. Ireland also had a cultural revival, expressed through its music, arts and thirst to recapture their own history and control of education. Already Ireland is planning its embassy in Scotland in anticipation of closer political links with the Scottish Parliament in Edinburgh. How long Labour expects to lower the Scots expectations with "just another English Parish Cooncil" in a disused Tory Brewer's building in Edinburgh, is anybody's guess. But we know whose side the Middle class English educated Great British left will be on. Don't we? We have seen the result of their North British auxiliaries playing the old colonial game, by trying not to be associated with the rest of the natives. Just like their colonial counterparts and gombeens in Ireland, India and elsewhere throughout the Evil Empire they seek to ingratiate themselves with their colonial masters.

"Ooh Ah, Up the Raj!"
"We Don't Need No Scottish Educashun. We're Just Another Brick in the Wall"

William Neill

Waste O Guid Siller

Provost MacPlook thinks that we maun caa doun — must knock down
thrie oot o fower colleges; faur mair — three, four
fushionless blethers ti be gotten thare — empty chatter
nor onie drucken Setternicht in toun. — than, drunken, Saturday night
A waste o siller pittin quine an loun — money, boy and girl
ti chauve et buiks until thair heids are sair; — drudge, sore
litterae humaniores, thowless fare - — ineffectual
aa yon fantoosherie o kep an goun. — flashy nonsense, cap and gown

Thir wastrife kickmaleeries in the schuils: — wasteful trifles
wheetlin recorders, tootlin clarinets-
confine aa kists-o-whistles ti the kirk. — organs, harmoniums etc.

Stick, says MacPlook ti *Hou ti Mak Oot Bills,*
Hou ti Wecht Tatties, Profit Ower Debts-
drap leirit falderals for honest wark. — scholarly

Mind Yir Taes — look out for your toes

(Dangerous objects dumped carelessly off the Solway coast began to be washed ashore)

Jist aff the Mull thare's s muckle howe in the sea- — large hollow
Atween the Scottish an the Irish shore
Some deep-doun girnel hes been caad ajee. — larder, torn apart
It skails oot shells that werna thare afore: — spreads
No clabbie-doos or buckies or siclike — mussels, whelks, suchlike
That ye micht byle an fry an eat wi saut. — boil, salt
Yon hairst that boaks up frae the Beaufort Dyke — harvest, vomits up
Ye winna swage, een wi the best o maut — digest, malt (whisky)
Dinna gae soomin doun bi Ballantrae — swimming
Or paiddlin near Portpaitrick – tell the wean - — child
Waur nor a scowder-stang thay'll gie ye pain. — Jelly-fish sting
Nae maitter who – thay're ower faur awa
ti kittle taes doun in Westminster Haa. — tickle toes

114

Cairnstanes

Whiles I gae by yon muckle cairn o stanes
wi gravit letters. Fowks aye come tae gant
an dinna ken preceislie whit they want
ither then trampin ower the poet's banes
or walkin twa yairds nearer his remains
gey near as if he wes some haulie saunt.
But fine we ken that sic a skellie sklent
Wad haurdlie fit this bard, for aa thair sains.

Wha wad jalouse he dee't gey fasht wi debt
an aa the Gret Fowk turnt thair nebs awa?
Echt geenies, sae I'm tellt, an nane cam near,

tae pey the chairge. Oor poet graned an swat
an feart for wife an bairns pit til the law.
It micht as weill be a cuddie yirdit here.

James D. Young

The Legacy of John MacLean Past, Present and Future

The three separate themes of the past, present and future of John MacLean(1879-1923), the world famous Clydeside socialist, 75 years after his death, should highlight what connects his life, times and legacy in 1998 to a present characterised by retrogression or counter-revolution and the really unpredictable future in the 21st century. With the exception of some maverick historians, most academic historians in the Scottish Universities insist on separating the past from the present at the same time as they refuse to speculate about the future. I am an 'old-fashioned' radical, not a maverick or conventional academic.

However, by inclination as well as conviction I am just as much a writer as I am a socialist or radical in Karl Marx's sense of the word radical. It was Marx who argued that to be 'a radical' means going to 'the root', and that 'the root is man'. So we must try to see the now hidden connections between MacLean's own life and times, the depressing world of the late 20th century, and the possibility at least of a genuinely Scottish-International radicalism in the next century.

In his book *Confound the Wise (1942)*, Nicolas Calas, Greek Trotskyist and surrealist poet, provided some excellent signposts suggesting how we could connect the past, present and the future from the vantage-point of a radical vision of the world. In that book he said that 'the best historians are those writers who know what they want the future to be'. He insisted that the 'future is part of the past', and that what we want must be in the 'future'. In a key sentence challenging post-modern pessimism and all the fashionable 'doom and gloom' propaganda about the premature burial of socialism – he argued that: *If we do not believe in the prospects of the future, perhaps because we expect them to be blacker than the past, then we must try to revive modes of life of that part of the past we remember.*

John MacLean would have had no trouble in accepting this approach to history.

The main outlines of MacLean's biography are now quite well known, though the elements of continuity and discontinuity in his life and thought as a socialist before and after 1917 remain much more obscure.

The first critical point to be made is that MacLean was a highly intelligent school teacher and socialist activist rather than a theorist or heavy weight writer of learned tomes. Unlike their leading English counterparts, the Scottish socialists of MacLean's time were poor. As a thinker MacLean was not a Rosa Luxemburg; and he spent so much agitating that he did not have the time or leisure to write books.

However, before 1914 he contributed weekly articles to *Justice*, organ of the Social Democratic Federation (SDF) – the first Marxist organisation in Britain. He was a British socialist and internationalist before the so-called 'war to end all war'. When he wrote about the radical uprising of 1820, he was simply not aware of any Scottish dimension. Indeed, he praised Baird, Hardie and Wilson – the 1820 martyrs – for struggling to get working-class Members elected to the House of Commons to represent the interests of the working class.

In the critical year of 1914 all Scottish socialists joined together to rubbish and ridicule the celebration of the 1314 Battle of Bannockburn. MacLean characterised the Battle of Bannockburn as a battle fought by serfs on behalf of a 'few barons'. Unlike John Carstairs Matheson, in some ways the major Scottish Marxist thinker and writer before 1914, MacLean did support the agitation for Scottish Home Rule. He also objected to the fact that there was not a 'single Scottish representative' on the national committee of the (British) SDF. His chief and best-known personal qualities were compassion for the 'underdog', integrity, and independence of mind.

The so-called 'Great War' transformed MacLean. When he was in prison in 1917, before his internationally famous 1918 trial in Edinburgh for his anti-militarist and anti-recruitment speeches, he began to think about James Connolly and the Irish question, his ancestors' experiences in and eviction from the Scottish Highlands and the need for Scottish Home Rule. Then he was inspired by the 1917 Bolshevik revolution; and his tactic of deepening the struggle for

117

national independence was to make trouble at home by trying to accelerate the break-up of the British Empire.

MacLean was, of course, influenced by his sense of identity as a Scot as well as his intense consciousness of his Marxism and internationalism. Unknown to most historians, or to MacLean, there was a battle in the SDF between 1894 and 1901 about the Irish and the Scottish national questions. This fight involved the English imperialist socialist H. M. Hyndman on the one hand, and James Connolly, Jim Connell, author of *The Red Flag*, and William Gee, Nairn on the other.

When Connolly went to Dublin in 1896 and formed the Irish Socialist Republican Party, Hyndman raised merry hell because James Connolly did not form an Irish branch of the SDF. But Connolly was guilty of much greater heresy than that. Hyndman explained that 'talk of winning complete separation from all connection with the British Empire sounds a bit out of place in a socialist manifesto'.

The dominant figure in the SDF did not stop there. So when Connolly tried to affiliate the Irish Socialist Republican Party to the Second International, Hyndman vetoed the application and the Irish socialist had no further dealings with the SDF. Connolly was isolated in Dublin and had no connection with MacLean or author of *The Red Flag,* Jim Connell . And yet Connell upset Hyndman, Harry Quelch and other pro-imperialist English leaders of the SDF by asking them to publish his pamphlet *Brothers at Last: An Appeal to Celt and Saxon,* celebrating the uprising of the United Irishmen in 1798.

Hyndman and company were upset by Connell's denunciation of imperialism in the Empire and of the murder of countless Black people. Then the Independent Labour Party in Glasgow, where he was living and earning his crust, agreed to publish *Brother at Last;* and, though he remained a member of the SDF, he asked the ILP to 'place on its programme National Independence for Ireland'. Then in 1901, when MacLean was an apprentice rank-and-file member of the SDF, William Gee told the annual conference of the SDF in London that the Scots would raise *The Red Flag* in Scotland before it was raised in England.

The Scottish socialists were more sympathetic to the Irish question than were their counterparts in the English socialist movement; and, if MacLean had known about the disputes between Hyndman and

Connolly, Connell and Gee, perhaps the history of socialism in Britain might have been very different. And Royden Harrison has argued that historians should be interested in what did not happen in history.

More of an internationalist and anti-racist than ever before, in 1917 MacLean became known as a major international figure: he had been a jail-bird, an advocate of socialism from below and a critical supporter of the Bolsheviks. The Communist Party of Great Britain(CPGB)was formed in 1920; but he refused to join it. And that was the rub: the origin of all the nonsense about his 'insanity'.

One reason for MacLean's refusal to join the CPGB was the Scottish national question; and in passing it should be noted that between 1919 and 1923 there was a heated debate in the early British communist movement about the Scottish question. But there were other reasons – the reasons of a Clydeside man of principle, a man who was anti-racist and anti-imperialist.

The leaders of the early CPGB were, in MacLean's eyes, guilty of a serious sin of omission, that is, of not opposing the First World War. None of them was sympathetic to James Connolly or to the Easter Rising in Dublin. And they were pro-imperialist. Indeed, at the Second Congress of the First International, Tom Quelch told Lenin that they could not support black struggles or anti-colonial revolts since the English workers would regard anything weakening the British Empire as 'treachery'.

The Legacy

One aspect of MacLean's legacy was the support for anti-racism, anti-imperialism and revolutionary socialism in the ILP in Scotland as distinct from its counterpart in England. The Scottish socialists – who should not be confused with the working class as a whole – were also more inclined to 'direct action' at the grassroots and to extra-Parliamentary politics. The latter tradition was set by MacLean when, in 1907, he asked unemployed workers to march across the floor of the Stock Exchange in Glasgow to highlight the problems induced by poverty and unemployment.

Moreover, after MacLean's death the CPGB became numerically stronger and ideologically more influential in Scotland than anywhere else in Britain. This pernicious Stalinist cultural orientation in the

Scottish labour movement remains formidable – a cultural conservative bulwark shored up by New Labour's continuation of the Thatcherite revolution and disgusting talk about the need to return to 'the actually existing socialism'. And this is a good pathway into discussing the present.

The Present

Our own times should have convinced socialists of the moral rottenness at the heart of contemporary capitalism. Unemployment; naked poverty; inadequate health care; the growing gap between the well-off and the unemployed and women and men who are paid dirt-cheap wages or sweeties; racism and the revival of fascism in conditions of economic scarcity: all these have combined to raise questions about capitalism. The propaganda of the New World Order communicates the 'common sense' idea that free-market forces – i.e. global capitalism – will work. But for whom do they work, and for how much longer can capitalism survive?

In contrast to the past – in contrast to MacLean's time – the genuine democratic, class-struggle Left is no longer in ascendancy. Day in and day out working people everywhere are told that we have reached 'the End of History' and that socialism – all visions of socialism – have been buried beyond any possibility of resurrection. In contrast to the past the Left is isolated, often defeatist; and socialists do not speak or write as thy did in the 1930s about *Why You Should Be A Socialist* or *The Coming Struggle for Power.*

And yet the arguments for international socialism have never been more compelling or more difficult to refute in rational debate. In the midst of this situation historians like Kenneth Morgan and Christopher Harvey rubbish MacLean and the real Scottish national question. So does a so-called Trotskyist like Bob Pitt. But in asserting that MacLean was 'insane' because he advocated Scottish national independence, refused to join the CPGB and formed the Scottish Workers' Republican Party, Pitt ignores the fact that even some of the Scottish Prison doctors refused to certify MacLean as 'insane'. Moreover Pitt ignores the fact that the Scottish prisons were, according to Peter Petroff, the Russian Bolshevik, worse than those in Tsarist Russia.

What is missing from the discussion about MacLean's alleged mental instability is any international context. When the Spanish anarchist Francisco Ferrer, was put on trial in Spain in 1909, he was characterised as 'insane' because he was an anarchist. Despite Ferrer's world prominence as a rational, Freemason and educationalist, he was buried in a common ditch after being shot by a military firing squad.

In 1919 Rosa Luxemburg was declared 'insane', and buried in a pauper's grave in Berlin. When the Nazis came to power in 1933 bulldozers were sent in to level the graveyard. Similar things were done in the 1920s in a Russia without soviets or workers' councils. In the early 1920s, too, Sacco and Vanzetti, the American anarchists of Italian origin, were declared 'insane' by the American authorities, and Vanzetti was jailed in a mental hospital. Unfortunately, by not sketching in such an international dimension, Pitt and his friends are contributing to the existing mood of pessimism and defeatism in socialist ranks. This is the most serious question facing the Left in 1998; and it can only be solved in struggles in which a radical vision will be developed and sharpened.

What, then, is left of the MacLean legacy? In my pamphlet *John MacLean: A Reply to Bob Pitt,* there is detailed account of MacLean's enduring influence on popular culture, including novels. Besides, without entering into the debate about 'heroes' and icons, we should ask ourselves why ruling classes treated Ferrer, Luxemburg, MacLean and Sacco and Vanzetti as they did and why the hacks today continue to rubbish their memory.

The real importance of MacLean for 1998 is that he offered people a radical vision of the better world to come. By fostering a radicalism of the mouth, an undue emphasis on the importance of Parliamentary politics instead of extra-Parliamentary 'direct action' and the myth of progress, the Stalinists and their 'actually existing socialism' have helped to destroy MacLean's vision of authentic socialism from the bottom up.

There have been other times in world labour history when the socialist vision has departed from socialists' consciousness. MacLean admired and was close to the Wobblies or members of the Industrial Workers of the World. In his novel *From Here to Eternity (1952),* James Jones said: *There has never been anything like them before or since. They called themselves materialist-economists but what they really were was a religion. They were workstiffs and bindlebums like you and me, but they were welded together by a vision we don't posses.*

Although struggles for social justice and democratic control will develop during the next few years, the genuine Left's critical and crucial role in the world at large is to expand solidarity and, above all, popularise its uncompromising *vision* of a radical egalitarian Scotland within a socialist world.

Two of the best radical books I have read in recent years have been *Culture and Imperialism (1993)* and *Beyond Capital (1995)* by Edward Said and by Istvan Meszaros. One of the best pictures of a future socialist Britain was *News from Nowhere (1890)* by William Morris; and it was a Utopian novel in which he envisaged the House of Commons and Palace of Westminster being used as places for the storage of dung or manure. Far from socialism being inevitable, the 'common ruin of the contending social classes' is a bigger danger than when Marx wrote those words in 1848.

However, if the world survives, it will be because socialists succeeded in developing a radical vision of a new global socialism free of inequality, poverty and oppression. Contrary to what authoritarian advocates of socialism from above have always argued, mean and ends cannot be separated. And radical visions, as Meszaros has argued, will be born inside the struggles against the New World Order.

When he wrote just after the British general election of 1992, Meszaros focused on the worldwide re-emergence of the national question. Attacking what he called the collapse of the Mickey Mouse socialism that coincided with the Labour Party's defeat in the general election of 1992 and the opening of Euro-Disneyland, he depicted some of the forces of disaffection and revolt. As he explained: *When Parliamentary expectations are bitterly disappointed people move in the direction of taking action. We had a very dramatic case in the recent past with the opposition to the Poll Tax. And now in Scotland people are talking about direct action, even civil disobedience, in order to assert what they consider to be their legitimate interest of securing their own parliament or even independence.*

In the misery and struggles of today lies the hope for tomorrow.

The Future

The myth of progress remains a dangerous one. In the circumstances of what is happening in various parts of the world, we should remember that Voltaire described history as 'a House of Funerals', and that Hegel saw the historical process as 'a slaughter-bench'.

When he discussed the origins of 'the inequality' of humankind, Rousseau wrote: *The first man who enclosed a piece of ground, bethought himself of saying 'This is mine', and found people simple enough to believe him, was the real founder of civil society. From how many crimes and murders, from how many horrors and misfortunes might not anyone have saved mankind, by pulling up the stakes, or filling up the ditch, and crying to his fellows, 'Beware of listening to this impostor, you are undone if you once forget that the fruits of the earth belong to us all, and the earth itself to nobody.'*

In a socialist world there will be no 'unfree' market forces or private ownership of land or the means of production.

In a sustained discussion and description of socialism in the future, in *Literature and Revolution (1925)* Trotsky said: *Life will cease to be elemental, and for this reason stagnant... The shell of life will hardly have time to form before it will burst open again under the pressure of new technical and cultural inventions and achievements. Life in the future will not be monotonous.*

But, although private capitalism was abolished in Russia after 1917, the dominance of **Capital** under totalitarian Stalinism thwarted the growth of any recognisable socialism. Any vision of a radical Scotland will have to repudiate any idea of 'socialism in one country'. Radicals will need to stress that socialism must become thoroughly internationalist and global without distinction of creed, colour or sex. So just as the new radical movements of the Left will need increasingly to become multicultural, so a future global socialism will offer the vision of an emancipated humankind radiating all the colours of a beautiful rainbow.

John Taylor Caldwell

Never Again

If had started work as a messenger boy or a van boy, instead of a cinema page, there would have been this difference: I would have worked more sociable hours and have been able to mix with young people of my own age and take part in back-street life at juvenile level, though I would have been something of an oddity among them. Whatever advantages that may have had, there would have been one deprivation. I would have missed the educative influence the screen gave. Although my deep introspections were of an abstract nature, concerned with the why and wherefore of existence, I was not unaware of what was happening on the earthly plane, nor was I disinterested. Whatever caused the phenomenon of life, here was the phenomenon of reality, every bit as much a mystery and a source of concern and perplexity.

With growing frequency I slipped from my post during the quieter matinee period, the doorman pretending not to notice, and went into the cinema to watch the films, which in those days were silent. Most of them were of American values and attitudes. Despite that, a wider world was opened to me in the presentation of life: of love, hate, heroism, ambition and frustration.

I ignored what I considered trashy romantic love stuff. Rudolf Valentino held no attraction for me, except in The Four Horsemen of the Apocalypse, which was an epic. I particularly liked historical pictures. I could merge myself into any period and any location and into most characters – I am generously endowed with sympathetic qualities. That which had been, on which the light of life had dawned, and whose sun had set, could be gathered within me and brought to life again; so was my own life extended and enriched. I never extended my lease of life by projecting it into the future. The future was lifeless; no amount of imagination would put blood into its veins and make its emotions real.

The recent war – the greatest of all time – supplied much material for the silent screen, drawing both the horror-seeking and the nostalgic. For a teenage boy, it supplied the excitement that violence inspires.

Most men I knew watched, but scoffed at these films with the authority of experience. They sneered at Yankee glamourization and chauvinistic glorification. The Germans were portrayed as cruel and stupid, gleefully perpetrating atrocities. The Allies (which meant the Americans, with an occasional glimpse of the British and even rarer view of the French) were good clean American boys, with a few endearing good-natured tough guys, like Victor McLaglen, recently imported from London.

The war was still a present spectre in the lives of most adult people. Its aftermath was still being felt, and with increasing intensity. Along the kerbs of many cities beribboned and bemedalled figures stood, scraping a violin, blowing a flute, or just holding a receptive cap. There were demonstrations, strikes and lock-outs. On walls and roadways were thick pipe-clay chalkings: *"WAR IS MURDER", "WAR IS HELL", "NEVER AGAIN"*.

My endorsement of that sentiment was passionate. I was congenitally opposed to violence. My wonderment at life rebelled against its impairment by debilitating circumstance or violence, and at its destruction by aggression. Experience at home, at school and in the streets of Belfast endorsed that basic instinct. This was further stressed by my own workmates who had served in the war.

One of these men, a survivor of the Somme, now a ticket-collector earning thirty shillings a week, less insurance, had constantly to wear surgical stays from chest to groin, having been ripped open by a bayonet. He had been sewn up, but the flesh had not joined properly and it was feared that any undue strain would rip him apart. He said that it had happened when he was lying already wounded and helpless in a shell-hole. He told the story without bitterness or grievance, and even enjoyed the doubtful importance it gave him.

There was bitterness and sadness, not against the Hun but against war itself, in a story told by another of the men, an Englishman in his mid-forties. His bitterest memory was of having to take part in the execution of an eighteen-year-old deserter. The story he told me was confirmed many years later in a book by judge Anthony Babington, giving an account of the young soldiers executed by firing squad during the First World War. My workmate did not tell the story in company; it was too painful for public exposure, but it probably gave him some relief to recall the experience to a young boy, when we were alone in the staff room.

The young soldier had panicked in the face of the enemy and had run away. He was found by a Frenchman, hiding in a stable, and was dutifully handed over to his regiment, where he was court-martialled and sentenced to death. My workmate told me:

"The boy was put in a tent, with the chaplain to give what comfort he could. All night we heard him weeping and asking for his mother. In the first light of morning he was brought out in front of a hedge beside a newly-dug grave. Every one of the firing squad's rifles was loaded with a live bullet – not, as is often supposed, just one live bullet and the rest blanks. The boy was blind-folded. The young captain in charge drew his sword, raised it, lowered it. We fired. The impact of the bullets almost cut the youth in two across the chest. He was slid, still warm, into the grave. The chaplain uttered a few words. The young body was covered in earth, and we were dismissed. The captain went on sick leave, and never returned.

My friend – I've forgotten his name – went on to tell me that shortly after that incident he had been taken prisoner by the Germans.

"They marched us, arms raised, several miles to a transit camp, kicking the colonel on the backside to humiliate him in front of his men. We were kept overnight in the camp, then packed into railway trucks, standing against one another, unable to move. The journey seemed to last for hours. We were ordered out. It was bitterly cold, with hard snow on the ground. Waiting for us was a crowd of German women with buckets of cold water and full chamber pots, which they emptied over us with much abuse. We were packed into open lorries and taken to a prisoner-of-war camp. There we were served our first meal of the day, a cabbage soup served in spittoons, which they must have collected for the purpose. They'll not get me next time, you may be sure of that. Never again!"

"Never again" expressed the mood of the people in general, and it impressed itself on my mind.

David Craig

The Rape and Old Age of Morag

She sees him out of the corner of her eye –
She turns to face him – he has hidden again
Behind the angle of the lambing-pen.
She sees him in silhouette against the sky
Where sandstone bulges like a dinosaur.
She sees him in the fox-head on the fence,
Rows of triangular quartz-white teeth that clench.
She sees him blocking the oblong of the door.
She sees him in the raven-hair that gleams
On the close-cut rounded head of her little son.
She sees him through the barrel of a gun
Eyeing her down its spiralling oily sheen.
She sees him in the midden, tapering red.
And in the stain above her single bed.

What had he said to her, the night he forced her,
Then slithered from the bedclothes, wiping his legs?
'Breathe a word and they'll turn you out to beg.'
Next he had tried to win her round with banter,
Bringing his pink lips inches from her ear:
'Cheer up, Morag! You mustn't look sad!
Like me a little, girl – I'm not all bad.
Why should a bit of fun end up in tears?'
Feeling his 'loving' touch she bit his hand,
Gagged on his taint of brandy and cigarettes,
Panicked for fear her blood had stained the sheets,
Started to feel her irreversible wound,
And still said nothing, making herself not cry.
But if she had a baby, she would die.

They moved to a stony croft along the coast,
Father and Mother, Morag and little Don.
In early July, when the clipping work was done,
She went to the shore and put him to her breast,
Feeling his small lips tickle for the milk.
Out in the loch the ebb had bared the rocks.
The drying weed was ticking like a clock,
The idle water stretched as grey as silk
Towards America. She would take the boat,
Put milk in a bottle, cuddle Don in his shawl.
Maybe they'd drown in the whirl of the overfall
Where Cailleach Bheur rinsed through her sodden clout.
Maybe the three white Birds of Bride would come,
Swathe them in bog-cotton, carry them home.

The minister arrived in a blast of hail.
'Desperate, desperate for the time of year!
I had great trouble getting up from the shore.
How are you all? And how is the little – ' Wail
Upon wail was greeting him from the corner crib.
The family stared at him, and on and on
The kettle stayed unboiled, the soda scone
Unmargerined. He lurched towards the babe,
His black coat flapping. Mother's voice came low:
'You can do nothing for us, bless or curse,'
And Morag carried Don upstairs to nurse,
Hating the man of God, who had tried to do
That thing which her own father had never done
And never would – give comfort to her son.

Always he seemed to be sitting underwater,
Father in Grandpa's chair beside the range.
On thundery mornings when the light was strange
He would stare as though he had never seen his daughter.
Dark in the Black Watch Tartan in his picture
Taken the month before he went to France,
He was the man who never had a chance
To escape from a life he saw as pure affliction.

When Uncle poached a salmon, he refused
To touch it, saying 'That was not *meant* for you.'
Two speeches she remembered, only two,
From all the condemning, judging words he had used:
'Always remember, Morag, what you have done.'
'It would have been *safer* if we had had a son.'

When Don was three, she took him to the haven
Where red rock parted to let in the tide
To the very lip of the croft. On either side
Rose sharp towers looming like the Prow of Blaven
Across the Inner Sound. Beneath the glistening
Pane of a tidal pool a sunken garden
Of seaweeds blossomed. She felt her four years' burden
Slide from her back. She sang, and Don was listening,
'Row me across to the islands.' Limpet shells
Lay in the crevices – they gathered them,
Launched them like little boats and watched them skim
On choppy wavelets, grounding on the shoals
Of bladder-wrack, parting and sailing on.
When they looked up, the afternoon had gone.

Mother was watching when they went for eggs
To the rushes of the out-by; when she washed
His dirty bottom; watching as she brushed
His stiff black hair, or soothed his angry legs,
Lumpy from nettle-stings, with leaves of docken;
Watching them when she slapped his sticky fingers
Scarlet with stolen jam – till Morag's anger
Festered with questions that could not be spoken:
What are you watching, Mother? what are you seeing,
The brute's face surfacing in the little boy's?
A gentleman's temper in the bairnie's cries?
She ached with words in the centre of her being
And still said nothing. Neither of them spoke.
All words had foundered when her waters broke.

129

She saw the Lodge as hell now, lurking under
The humped, star-blotting outline of the Bheinn.
It was a kind of pit for dirty men.
A place where beasts and criminals would go
To build their torture-chambers. Over the years
Their cars got bigger, wilder music sounded
On August evenings. Then the place was blinded,
The windows shuttered. Brambles and rusting wires
Strangled the lords' and ladies' paradise.
They would be back, or foreigners would come
To fish and kill. It had never been a home,
The 'castle' in the forest, hidden from eyes
Of visitors and crofters, where the swine
Mounted each other, drowned in tubs of wine.

When Donald was gathering buckies on the shore
With Uncle's red-haired twins from Allt-na-Feidh,
She sat and listened, hiding in the lee
Of the Blaven-towers. She heard the redheads swear:
'Bugger off, Donny! The biggest ones is mine.'
'*You* bugger off!' A howl of grief – a splash
Flat as the down-fall of a jumping fish.
She rose to her feet – heard little Angus whine,
'Leave me alone. And leave my brother be,
You filthy bastard.' Not a word from Don.
Then, 'I'm not crying. I'll never cry again.
None of you's big enough to frighten me.'
A little later, 'I'll fight you both.' And once,
'I'm crying because my Dad was killed in France.'

Mother was dying of tuberculosis.
Her voice came maundering from the upper room:
'Never ask for money! When'll he come?
Morag my darling, your cheeks are pink as roses...'
Where should she go, to the road at Tigh-na-Greíne
Where neighbours were, the postie and the nurse?
She could not face them. Allt-na-Feidh was worse –
Uncle was there – the mountains stood between –

The waters would boil a thousand feet below –
Don would delight in it – her head would reel
With the white swirling, like the path to school
On days of spate, eleven years ago...
She sat, and Mother cried out overhead,
Spilling her last blood on her marriage-bed.

They settled into their days. Their long days turned
Like swathes beneath the scythe. The channel flowed
Into the loch and out again. Like roads
The tidal currents shimmered blue, or burned
To embers at the close of another year.
In sultry July the twins would come and clip –
Straightening their backs to watch a distant ship,
Cracking a sheep-tick on the collie's ear –
Then left 'to earn good wages' down the coast.
Don was immune to money, took his rod
And disappeared behind Bheinn Ruadh-side.
She rarely saw him watching for the post.
His world was all inside him, turned down low,
Listening to Irish on the radio.

Once when he went to Perth to buy a dog
He passed through Kyle, stood on the harbour wall
And watched the shingle under-water crawl
And teem with feeding crabs. He *heard* the drag
And clack of avid pincers, felt them close
On crumbs of flesh, saw the plate-armoured back
Of the one great crab-animal print its black
On a white carcass lying in the ooze.
It was like looking into a brain and seeing
The layered thoughts stir with a pulse of pain or fear.
Maybe his father's remains were lying there –
Maybe it was like that when he was dying
'Lost in the Gulf' soon after he had 'gone
To Texas' and would be 'sending for them soon'.

He was himself whenever he took his rod
Far up behind Bheinn Ruadh to a lochan
Dark as a starless night, its glaze unbroken
By any gull or otter. It lay hid
Below a buttress and a tottering stack.
Two trout would rise in a spellbound afternoon.
He would grow small and still as though he had been
Unborn again into the womb of rock.
He was himself when digging out a cairn.
Foxes had had the meat of forty lambs.
His terrier crawled back out, died in his arms
Matted in fox-blood, cradled like a bairn.
He was himself when Mother, clutching her head,
Told him his father raped her in her bed.

She sat in the home-made armchair, feeling her feet
Throb like two yeasty loaves about to rise.
She irked and hotched, trying to be at ease
Or Don would be furious, battering at the peats
With the auld fire-tongs. He was on the hill,
Levelling his telescope along his legs.
The sheep on the distant path were close as bugs
Grandpa had spoken of, clustering down his kilt
In pleated lines. He had tried to see his own
Face in the Black Watch photograph, his nose
Pinched at the nostrils, the meeting of his brows…
All that they had in common was the frown.
What was he? He was a person. He was one
Of a trillion blobs of life. He was a man.

Nobody dreamed that he would die before her.
She was familiar, white hair in the porch.
The men from Tigh-na-Greíne, off to catch
The crabs and lobsters or line for plaice off Morar,
Would wave to her – could she see them? Up on the slope
The tall, round-shouldered figure of her son
Would scythe the short hay, laying green on green,
Or stride with his dog and cromach after his sheep.

On the calm of a rainy day she still heard nothing
At eleven in the morning from his room.
She hirpled through to his bedroom in the gloom
And saw beneath the quilt no rise of breathing,
No crimp on his sunburnt forehead, not a trace
Of feeling in his stony-sculptured face

Where over and over she had looked for anger,
Some quirk of humour, or a blench of pain.
All this could not have vanished from his brain!
She beat on his chest with fists, with failing fingers,
With sweating palms that badgered and caressed.
Nothing. She took a sheet from the press and hung
It up in the pine tree. Before the day was done
The fishermen came to her through the mist
And carried Don to the haven. Like a spectre
One heron left the rocks and flapped off low.
Nobody said a word. They watched it go
On shrouding wings above the sluggish water.
Her heart broke then. She had nothing left to give.
Why should she be the one condemned to live?

She sees him close behind her, darkly reflected
In the window facing seaward, stooping outline
Superimposed on the washed turf of the shoreline,
Standing among the curlews, looking dejected.
She sees him in the hound's-tooth-check deerstalker
Hung on the hooks for Visitors. She sees him
In Father's photo. (What can she do to please him?)
She sees him the brown face of the doctor
Who called to give her 'something for her fever'
And listen to her heart. She sees his face
In the Sheltered Housing garden, in the space
She has made her own, while over and over and over
She counts the days they spent together alive:
Sixteen thousand two hundred and twenty-five.

John Manson

Scotland – National and International

My Scotland starts in the Thirties. Ian MacPherson's *Shepherds' Calendar* 1931 re-creates it best though his father was a factor in Forres and my father was a crofter in Caithness. It was published a year before I was born and the time is November 1925 to October 1926 on a holding in Fordoun.

Grassic Gibbon defines it best as '... this code of suppression...' in *Niger: The Life of Mungo Park*, '... his world of multitudinous sense-impressions superimposed with the most narrow and Spartan code of conduct ever invented outside Laconia', thinking, no doubt, of his own young days in Arbuthnott.

It was this 'code of suppression' that Hugh MacDiarmid broke out of in *'Charisma and My Relatives',* also published in 1931:

> No' here the beloved group; I've gane sae faur
> (Like Christ) yont faither, mither, brither, kin
> I micht as weel try dogs or cats as seek
> In sic relationships again to fin'
> The epopteia I maun ha'e – and feel
>   (Frae elsewhere) owre me steal.

These 'relationships' had become a kind of incestuous blackmail:

> But naewhere has the love-religion had
> A harder struggle than in Scotland here
> Which means we've been untrue as fechters even
> To oor essential genius – Scots, yet sweer
> To fecht in, or owre blin' to see where lay,
>   The hert o' the fray.

This is the kind of cowardice MacPherson and MacColla describe in *Shepherds' Calendar* and *The Albannach* respectively, the inability of their characters, John Grant and Murdo Anderson, to initiate, to take charge of their lives because of the weight of their parents' authority at the time of their powerlessness.

I first became aware of Scottish literature and language, and their relevance to my experience and to the experience of my forebears, when I was studying English literature and language at the University of Aberdeen.
My father had been conscripted in 1916; I read Grassic Gibbon's threnody for the armed gulags which clashed by day and by night in the 'holocaust in the fields of France'. My great-grandmother on his side had been evicted from Strathnaver at the age of three in 1819; I read Fionn MacColla's description of the Clearances and the debates on their causes in *And The Cock Crew*. My mother was a native of the islands of Stroma and had a considerable Norn content in her vocabulary.
But almost at the same time as I first read *Charisma and My Relatives* I also found that Franz Kafka had described something like the same kind of claustrophobic experience in different ways in another country and in another (original) language. Later I found that Barbusse and Remarque had also written about the 'holocaust in the fields of France'; Anna Seghers, Silone and Steinbeck had written about crises in peasant communities as well as Grassic Gibbon. The whole of human experience could not be re-created in one national literature. It was necessary both to break the hegemony of English literature in Scotland and to extend my reading to other literatures (which would include English). In Halldor Laxness' words I concluded that 'What is human is international'.
So in fiction now I think of a great variety of characters: George Heisler, who escapes from Westhofen in Anna Seghers' *The Seventh Cross;* the *okhlomons* (expelled Party members) who live in a lime kiln in Pilnyak's *Mahogany* and *The Volga Flows into the Caspian Sea;* the truculent labourers in Gorky's story, *At the Salt Marsh;* Andrejs Pikieris, the demagogic candidate for his own 'non-party party', who canvasses with a gramophone and a film-projector in Vilis Lacis' *A Fisherman's Son;* Peter Threehorse, the entrepreneur in Laxness' *World Light;* the high school girl graduates who act in a superior manner to a boy who is still at school in Pramoedya Ananta

Toer's *This Earth of Mankind* – as well as the Gourlays and Gillespie Strang.

And in the poetry of Louis Aragon, Manuel Bandeira, Paul Eluard, Eugenio Montale, Pablo Neruda, César Vallejo – as well as MacDiarmid and Sydney Goodsir Smith.

Scotland a nation – reaching out to all nations.

Albert Mackie said of Hugh MacDiarmid that 'he socht a Scotland sib and chief wi the warld wide, shakan a luif wi France and Russia, shouther to shouther wi forrit-leuken folk o aa lands, whether Jew or Gentile, black, white, or brown. That is the Scotland that is waukenan the day, that is the Scotland that will face the fecht o years to come....'

To An Unconceived Child

'My personality was crushed gradually, but surely,
and in imitation of life grew out like a derision
of everything which was sacred to me...'
N.M. Seedo, In the Beginning was Fear

On a night of wind and rain
The crofter used to hope
The lambs would 'stay where they were'

Stay where *you* are
In the egg
In the seed unmet
Until I am sure
You will never know
The debilitation of sin
Or the holiness of salvation

Or stagger without sound
In slow motion
From the gas chamber of prayer
Lethal to life
As a stunned fly

136

Drags his legs away
To a dark corner
No one looks by

Or live in the head
Live to work
Liking in nothing
Owning in the name of loving
An iron implement
Shouting psalms

The aamel wags at the tail o the plou
The horses pu on the chains
I to the hills will lift mine eyes

What language did I learn
On the Bass rock
Of a Caithness croft
Among the yithings and soughings
The subserviences
The shutting up
It was reported he spoke good Calvinese

The mear's lips
In the gowden sun

The act a thousand times hated once admitted
White seed spurting on white frost

The stirk's on his tether
And his baakie's doon

The hobbled horse
The coo in the branks
The yowe in her hems
The high jumper shackled

I am the seed under the stone
        the tree that grew out of the wall
        the spider that never reached the beam
        the stream that sometimes cracks the surface

The gress grows up
Around the stane
Bit in the mool
White ruit
Yella shuit

Christ wis lucky after aa
Some ane rowed the stane awa

*'Here guilt is with the innocent, the sacrificer
is the sacrificed...' Joseph Lengyel*

This is it then
We cannot annul
Let the demanders
Emotional blackmailers
And manipulators note
They told us it was right
It was right for themselves
And they won as they intended

Stay where you are
Until I am sure
You will never know
The suspicion of an unhinged woman
The distortion of placation
(In emotion, too, exploitation
Leads only to impoverishment)
The blame of your wrecker
A victim's conscience
The liberal who thinks
You may not be entirely to blame
The socialist who thinks
His understanding will surely make you conform

aamel – swingle-tree; yithings – lispings of 'yes'; baakie – iron spike for tethering an animal; branks – a
kind of bridle or halter with wooden side-pieces; hems – triangle (in the case of sheep)

Alex Cathcart

The Not-so-old Old Labourer

Alexander Mcfadden, MEP, West Central Scotland, was struggling forward, careful not to disturb the chauffeur, bending, loosening the shoelaces, seeking relief from the sun; that sun which would shine all the way from Frankfurt to Strasbourg and always right through the car window. Relief. And those two flymen who had been quick off the mark were sitting in the back, not even letting on they had noticed. Jackson, the Proles' real, real, friend, was pretending sleep. Quilm, champion of the city and the 'shire, with the accent that touched servile chords stuck down somewhere in the Mcfadden napper, unmoved, staring straight ahead. Flymen. In the shade.

McFadden had to curl up, against the car door, a try at giving the sun less target. Anyway; it was better that Jackson should be in the back with Quilm. That should ensure silence. Quilm would not talk to the madman of Strasbourg. And the madman of the Hemi-cycle would not speak to the man he called the non-person of the European Parliament. Non-person. Jackson giving away his roots there. This McFadden was too hot and fed up to talk to either of them.

Bloody heat. It was as hot in this car as the June night Alexander, nee Sandy, McFadden had been declared an unexpected winner. One minute a scaffolder, ah wait, a charge-hand right enough, the next, the next, a scaffolder no more. The bear is going to Strasbourg. Your man walked up the middle and got the job.

But some job. A job jumping off trains and planes, in and out of tubes, and cars, listening, nodding to the babble of tongues, and waiting; for tubes and cars and planes and debates and trains and votes and eats and people and a week to pass sleeping in strange, silent-walled hotel rooms, while a wife slept alone and the kids played cowboys by themselves. Should have had them earlier. Now Marjory coped as the kids got out of hand and Alexander, nee Sandy, grew fat. There was still some hardness to be felt. But it was more and more obvious. Muscles that once were hard, turning soft, turning fat. Fat was that. Not a stomach anymore. A belly. A wee roly-poly man that used to be a lean construction bear who could nip up and down scaffolds like a monkey on a tree and fling tubes and tubes about as if they were rods of hollow bamboo. Proud. A pride of scaffies. Working as a team. Rab and Bonzo would be up there somewhere on a day like today. Stripped to the waist. Working and balancing. Singing and joking and reaching down to catch the shackles on their way up,

"RIGHT BONZO"

The driver braked. Tyres squealed. Quilm came forward. Jackson was cursing and swearing in the only language he knew.

"Je suis pardon, monsieur, m , je regret, you know, j'eprouve du regret, I think."

The driver said nothing but spoke Esperanto with his face. Quilm only shook his head and settled back.

"What was all that about, Mr. McFadden sir?" asked Jackson.

"Nothing. Honest. I was dreaming and I just gave a shout. Sorry if I disturbed your beauty sleep."

"It's no me I'm worried about son. One minute you're the quiet man and the next you're screaming the place down. I think I'll have to have a word with that wee woman of yours. I'll see to it she gets you out in the fresh air."

Sometimes Jackson was better when he was silent. Fresh air, fresh air. Maybe that's what was needed. Loads of it. And people that know how to respond to your shouts. Fresh true air. Where your mates depended upon how you worked and would put their life on your word. When a scaffolding team said a job was done, it was done. No ifs, buts, qualifications; it was done. And a drink could be taken with an easy conscience and a laugh. Pissed if you like. No need to worry about the people peering over at you, over the chilled, white wine, and hanging on to every word, waiting for the one that would hang you.

"Passport, s'il vous plait?"

The border already. Not far now.

"Passeport?"

Bugger. "Oh. Sorry; its in my bag, sorry, oh, shit, j'ai perdu".

Quilm was leaning forward. Flashing his card. Deputé de Parliament Europeene. The French was flowing from his mouth. No effort. No hums, no haws. A pleased customs man was smiling and touching his cap. Quilm leaned out the window a little and said something. The officer smiled wider and nodded and looked down at the front seat passenger. Which was McFadden. What was he laughing and nodding at? Quilm was sitting up straight, knowing he looked the part, likely thinking McFadden was a clown because the French was rotten. Bloody rubbish. The bloke was like that all the time. Always tickety boo. Dress always correct. Hair always as if he'd just had it cut a week ago. Not ten days, but a week ago. Quilm was smiling. And McFadden wasn't. Jackson was laughing.

"What happened to the French there son? No point in them sending us all the way down to Cannes to learn it if you fall at the first hurdle."

"At least I tried."

"Sounds like your epitaph son."

The feet were still killing. But it would be as well to tie up the laces here. The car had turned right now. Past the coal docks. Little black hills of coal. There used to be hills of coal like that on the Glasgow docks; when Sandy McFadden was a name shouted to a mucky happy wee boy who played games among the coal wagons that brought the coal from the pits of Lanarkshire. Coal wagons that were fun but could take your leg off. No danger now. Now there were no pits. Now there were no wagons. Now there was no happy wee boy.

The car was heading down, following the blue signs with their circles of yellow stars. Down to the Palais D'Europe. Down past the narrow tenements with their curling balcony banisters and past the flash flats with their penthouses on top and there it was ahead, opposite the park where Napoleon had built the house for Josephine. One of the many he had built and she had never seen. And in Glasgow people lived in houses they wished they had never seen. But the driver changed his mind. He went on and turned across. He was taking them down the smaller entrance. They were there. Monsieur McFadden est arrivee. Arrive.

The guard in the little box on the other side of the street was laughing. No-one was near him. And he was laughing. Why shouldn't he laugh? Maybe that was the question. Why couldn't Sandy McFadden laugh. Maybe that was a clue. When was the last time Alexander McFadden had genuinely laughed? Truly, genuinely laughed? People used to say wee McFadden had a hearty laugh, even a dirty laugh, a kind of laugh that made other people laugh. A laugh like a youngster sinking up to his ankles in coal dust while big sister called him away and threatened to tell Mammy. Happy like the lad sitting under the kitchen table listening and watching a whole load of people singing and drinking and dancing and laughing, laughing, just because it was New Year.

Alexander McFadden took the bag from the chauffeur, turning, taking another look at the guard. The sentry's eyes were aimed up high somewhere as he saw and laughed at the picture in his mind's eye. Jackson was speaking. That guard was bloody happy about something. Jackson was saying something.

"See the old Euro flag's at half-mast."

Quilm responded to the puzzled tone of voice. "Somebody must be dead. Can't recall having read anything over the weekend."

Jackson laughed, but not as naturally as the guard. He laughed the politician's laugh. The laugh Alexander McFadden could do. Jackson lifted his suitcase. "Don't kid yourself, son. It's drooping for democracy. Simple democracy. C'mon, McFadden, you here for the day?"

They went in past the familiar faces of the security men who tried to appear as if they were not studying these familiar faces.

The office; the same as it had been left. Bare desk, empty, empty chairs. The earphones had fallen on the floor. The bags were thrown on the couch. As usual the window had to be opened. The rumour was that the Palais was a sick building.

In front, the rooftops of Strasbourg stretched out, the spire of the Gothic cathedral rising above all. Below, the guard still stood, tiny in his box. Just around the corner from him a lorry was unloading scaffolding tubes onto the ground, next to an old house. Looked like a renovation job. Two men working on the scaffold, building it up around the house. Two men only. Should be three, judging by the gear. Definitely a three man job. Maybe working a fiddle on the costing. Maybe the third man was helping unload the lorry.

The two were working well. Standards were up. Ledgers were getting fitted quickly. They were good. That was quite a complicated cathead they had slung up already. They must have started early. Quite mathematical. None of your unit frame stuff here. Two of the old school. But there should be three.

Something was going on in the Hemi-cycle. Tinny noises were emanating from the headphones. Alexander McFadden turned away from the scaffolding, bent, and picked up the earphones that linked him in to the debating chamber. The earphones had been left tuned in to the French. He sat down, twiddled the knob, and there it was in the English.

142

Deputé McFadden was missing a debate on some motion about funding for cultural workers. Why not? Candles in the garret must be indefensible with all the food mountains piling up that high the artists would soon be able to open the garret window and help themselves.

Whatever had caused the excitement couldn't have been much. Perhaps someone had found a cheaper way to travel to Strasbourg. No. That would have kept the chattering going until midnight.

Travel meant distance. Distance. A phone call to Marjory might help. Leave it leave it leave it leave it. Leave it for tonight. Nights were lonelier.

The door was opening. Jackson. "You in?"

"Billy. Come in. I was just thinking about taking a walk over to the Hemi-cycle, see what we're in for this week. What time's the Group meet?"

"Not till tomorrow. I've only come in to ask you if you've got a copy of De Vile's report on Consumer Studies? You got one?"

"Nope. Sorry, Billy, he's not on my Committee. Sorry old son."

"Ach, don't worry, I'll get one from publications, they'll probably be glad to get rid of another one." Jackson rose and nodded cheerio.

Cheerio, "That you? Just in, right out. Can you never sit still for a blether?"

"Whole place is for blethering, old son. I'll need to go Al. Sorry."

"That's O.K. Where are you eating tonight?"

"I've got one of these lobbying dinners to go to: IBM I think it is. Some folk going I want to see anyway."

"Saves you buying yourself a dinner you mean."

Make him stay. Say Something.

"I thought at least you might have wanted to get your wee dig in about my deselection."

" I never boot a man when he's down, son. Unlike your pals at Keir Hardie."

"O.K for you. You're retiring."

"No room for unreconstructed, aged Labourites with this mob Al. I've had enough of this anyway, so I thought I'd jump and not give them the satisfaction."

"At least they were gunnin' for you for some political reason, the bastards spun it out that I don't have, what was it, quite as much talent as others'.Cheeky bastards. And I'm supposed to swallow that."

"Aye, I seen that in the papers. I thought that was a bit under the belt, even for this shower. Well, if you keep a hush, they just might select you for the Scottish Parliament. You can maybe get a wee seat in there. If you're a good boy."

"They're Stalinist bastards."

"Oh, no, no, tut, tut, I'm the Stalinist. Anyway you can always go back to the buildings. Get your money honourably."

"Ach. I'm no fit for that anymore."

"Well, if you ever fancy helping me and the other dinosaurs rebuild the Party, you're welcome aboard. There's a lot to be done. We live in exciting times. I mean, there's so few of us left that we even need people of your limited talent to help."

"Fuck off."

"Everybody seems to be saying that to me this weather. And now you too, Brutus."

"Ah cut it out. Look, I'll see you."

Jackson left and the door was closed over. Deputé McFadden swung from side to side in his swivel chair as if considering something tres important. But there were no thoughts in the mind. Alexander McFadden stood up, and turned to the window, looking to the outside.

The roofs of Strasbourg hadn't changed. The guard was out of his box, looking up, exchanging banter with the scaffolders as they worked. Still only the two scaffies.

The phone was lifted. Buttons hesitantly pushed. No answer. Marjory was probably at the shops. Or her mother's. Whatever.

It was time to go, move about, look active. Maybe meet somebody.

There was no-one in the corridor. No-one at the lift. No-one in the lift.

The usual parade was passing along the walkway to the Hemi-cycle. Only Brit was him from Northern Ireland. Couldn't speak to him.

The messengers sat at their desks outside the chamber, and didn't lift their heads as Alexander McFadden passed them. Stopping inside the doorway to the chamber it was easy to see that a debate on cultural workers did not raise much excitement. Lots of blue empty chair spaces today. Not many Brits in.

A tap was being tapped on the shoulder. The man dressed as a penguin was leaning forward, making his big gold locket dangle. "Monsieur?" Equals: who are you?

"Deputé"

"Pardon?"

"Je suis Deputé"

"Oh" Equals: you could have fooled me.

The vote would be getting called soon. Best to get away. Vote or no vote, it would make little difference to the outcome. Everybody was for culture. Some people could never get enough of it. Some people liked culture because a cultured society was a job-creating society.

Deputé McFadden crossed over to the contact boxes at the edge of the circular landing. Nothing much in the box: a couple of notices of motion, but nothing substantial. Turning around he selected the week's work from the rack: one of these and one of these and one of these and one more and one more and at least it's something to read. At least with the papers Monsieur McFadden looked the part. Tres Important Personne. Like that one who carried the papers clutched to his chest as though a gale had sprung up and was threatening to blow them away.

The bar was tempting. But more people would only underline how few people were known. Even him from the BBC never wanted to talk to McFadden Who? But people were there, buzzing around, nattering here, nodding there. The usual fashion show: male and female model Europeans.

Maybe Marjory would be in.

The walk back was the same. Some French people were in the lift, but they spoke too fast. Office was the same. The view was the same. Still only the two.

Tres Important Papers were thrown on the desk. Phoning tried again. Marjory was still out. The grip on the receiver was tight, and the desire was to slam it down, but was resisted. It was replaced. The hands fell onto the lap. Fresh air.

On the way out slamming the door helped. Alexander McFadden was moving to some purpose: Get some fresh air.

Outside the building it was a clear, hot sun, cool blue sky day. Six deep breaths were taken. Familiar clanging and banging and scraping noises came from the scaffolders at work. A series of separate clangs and a solid bump sounded as one of the scaffolders dropped a tube from the top.

McFadden crossed over, to stand at the corner, looking. Moving closer, still looking. One of the scaffolders was struggling with a twelve-footer. Tired. Two into three does not go. McFadden came forward. The jacket was hung on a tube-end. McFadden was running at the ladder, hands and feet moving in co-ordination, rejoicing, glad to be called upon. No problem. Up the ladder, along the first platform , up to he next, along, skipping up the ladder, reaching the ledgers the scaffolders were working at. The scaffolder was still struggling. McFadden's feet were moving to balance. The dangling end of the twelve-footer was grabbed. "I've got it Bonzo." The scaffolder was frowning. "It's O.K. I've got it, mate. Let go, it's O.K., I'm a scaffolder, je suis, me, je suis, ach."

Alexander McFadden did not know the word for scaffolder. McFadden was getting angry. The tube was swung up, out of the man's hand, swung, easy, dead centre into the mouth of the shackle. "Gimme it. Gimme your key, your key. Clef. Clef."

The point and the gesture got the man to move, and he flung the spanner over to McFadden. With unbroken, unforgotten moves, McFadden caught it, closed the shackle, and tightened the clampnut. The French worker stepped along to his own end. McFadden watched, waited, threw him the key. And it was finished.

The Frenchman came toward him along the staging. He held out a hand. "Monsieur, dangereux. C'est très dangereux."

"Think I don't know?"

"The man wasn't following; he was scratching his head and his mate poked his head above the ladder. The two spoke rapidly, too fast. The second man finished with a clamber onto the staging. He carried sandwiches and a bottle of wine. The two sat down, their backs supported against the old house, they were gesturing for McFadden to do the same. Sandy pointed to the wine. "Dangereux, n'est-ce pas?

The lunch bearer waved a dismissive hand. "Le travail, c'est fini. Fini." McFadden sat down. As he got comfortable he looked towards the windows of the Palais D'Europe. Quilm was standing at his office window, scowling. McFadden put his arm around the shoulder of the nearest scaffolder.

"Hey, tell me, savez-vous L'Internationale?"

J. N. Reilly

an extract from
Raining Joy Blossoms

From the limpid disturbance
Refreshing rains
A sigh of dreams
Mysteries of bliss

The moment waking
Be, says the enchanting
Tender fingertips touching
A sweet moaning blossoming

Glasgow 1980

Vernon Coleman

Requiem for the NHS
On the Occasion of its 50th Birthday

If the NHS were a loved pet dog or cat (or a human being in a caring institution) it would have been put to sleep long ago. The NHS spirit died years ago. But no one has yet had the guts to bury the body – which is steadily decomposing. I use to believe in the NHS. Twenty years ago I objected strongly when friends chose to seek private medical treatment rather than use the NHS. Ten years ago I was still fighting for the NHS – although concerned about the quality of the treatment being provided for patients. But my idealistic objections to previously faithful patients betraying the NHS and having a bit on the side with the private health industry have gone. I now strongly advise everyone I know who is ill and

147

wants orthodox medical treatment to seek private medical care. Unless you want to die quickly and in great pain it really is the only sensible option. Only road accident victims, masochists and those too poor to do anything else trust themselves to the NHS these days. Even some NHS hospitals have given up pretending that they can provide a decent service. I know of NHS hospitals which now run an internal two tier service. If you want an appointment before you die you simply pay the hospital extra to see a consultant privately. A few years ago such a system would have seemed about as likely as the Church of England running weekday bingo sessions in St. Paul's.

The NHS has been killed by a combination of factors. The basic problem has always been the administration. NHS hospitals have always been absurdly over endowed with two life forms: cockroaches and administrators. The cockroaches are useful because they eat up bits of food that have been dropped on the floor. Successive governments have recognised the need to streamline the system and have fiddled with the structure. But the fiddling has been done by administrators and seems to have brought more new layers of administration. The staff who get their hands bloody – doctors, nurses, porters, technicians – have been gradually demoralised by knowledge that they are expected to cope in overcrowded, underfunded departments while thousands of vastly overpaid administrators have week long meetings on the Riviera to decide what colour carpet to put in the executive washrooms.

There is a widespread myth that the NHS is short of money. This is a lie of political proportions. The NHS is awash with money. But the stuff is wasted on pot plants, fancy furniture and obscene salaries for regiments of besuited men and women who contribute nought point zilch to patient care. The demoralised front line staff no longer care. Most are just working on to pay their mortgages. Retirement is their only passion. And so theft and deceit are commonplace. Hardly anyone gives a damn about patients anymore. Poor sods who put their lives in the hands of the NHS wait months for initial appointments. They then wait months to have tests done. And they wait months for the treatment they need. No one knows how many trillion patients die on these waiting lists.

As a doctor I have been embarrassed for years by the way patients are now treated within the NHS. I have heard of patients kept waiting for hours in outpatient departments because 60 people were all booked in at

148

2pm. Flat-bottomed patients then get two minutes with a junior doctor because the consultant who is paid to see them is sucking up to his private patients. The NHS lot think themselves lucky if the overtired junior doctor who sees them speaks more than two words of English. Patients wait six months for vital X-rays. They wait weeks before they are told the results of laboratory tests. None of this is excusable. It happens because no one gives a damn.

The NHS will never actually die in the body, of course. No politician would ever dare kill it off. And so it stumbles along: a headless, directionless monster, kept alive by summer fetes and bring and buy sales where local do-gooders gather together to raise cash to buy scalpels, bedpans and new bed linen. The innocent, the naïve and the well meaning fund raisers – not realising that every penny donated protects the corrupt system – will keep the whole sorry mess alive well into the 21st century.

Of course, the NHS could be saved. If I were Minister of Health I would abolish waiting lists and improve morale massively in just one week by doing two simple things. I would fire nine out of ten administrators (no one except the administrators would notice but the news would be received with whoops of joy by doctors and nurses). And I would tell hospital consultants that they had to choose between working for the NHS and working privately. The present absurd system allows many specialists to get the best of both worlds. Specialists deliberately keep their NHS waiting lists long so that patients are prepared to pay for private treatment. If specialists were forced to choose between the NHS and private work, most would opt for a nice fat regular NHS pay cheque. And waiting lists would disappear virtually overnight.

Sadly most UK politicians are cryptorchid and so none of them are likely to have the balls to take these two vital steps. There may be some who believe that the 50th anniversary of the NHS is a cause for celebration. I am not numbered among those innocents. In spirit the NHS died years ago. The shambling, disorganised, corrupt organisation which survives is a marriage between State and consumer which long ago fell apart; destroyed by the trusting naivety of one partner and the reckless, short-sighted greed of the other. The naivety of patients will doubtless be confirmed by the arrival on the editor's desk tomorrow of a shoal of letters from patients insisting that the NHS looked after them well. Such patients do, I suppose, have something to be proud of: they at least survived an encounter with the NHS. And that's more than many can say.

William Hershaw

Jimmy Sinclair – A Song

My name is Jimmy Sinclair,
I am a Fife born man,
My faither still talks o mining days
That are forty years lang gaun.
Aye, they're a' gaun nou, they're a' gaun nou.

A fitter in the Dockyard ,
When I was in my 'teens,
Bonuses and overtime
On nuclear submarines.
But they're a' gaun nou, they're a' gaun nou.

If I came fae the East Neuk
I would have gaun tae sea,
But buildin' rigs in Methil
Was the closest I could be.
And they're a' gaun nou, they're a' gaun nou.

I singed on in the eighties
When Thatcher ruled the roost,
Criminals made millions
While we lived fae hand tae mooth
And she's gaun nou, and she's gaun nou.

I was hoping for Hyunda
Nou they tell me "Wait and see"
Tell me, Mr Broon,

Whit will ye dae for me?
For it's a' gaun nou, it's a' gaun nou.

I voted for an assembly
And I'll vote for liberty,
I voted for New Labour
Though ma hert is S.N.P.
Whaur dae we gaun nou ? Whaur dae we gaun nou ?

I'm hameless and I'm jobless,
Withoot a cloot I stand,
Just like Piper Alpha
Disaster's near at hand.
For it's a' gaun nou, it's a' gaun nou.

History

As long as there shall but one hundred of us remain alive

As long as there shall but one hundred o   us remain alive

As long as there s all but one hun red o   us remain   live

A long as there shall but one   d ed o   us remain alive

A long a   there shall b   one hundred o   us remain live

As long as there shall b   e hundred o   us r   ain live

As   g as there shall b   e hundred of us   main   live

        l   as t ere   all   one hundred of us remain alive

A   l   a   ne hundred of us remain alive

A   l   as   here   all b   e   dred of us   ma n alive

A   l   as   there s all b   red of us   ain alive

A   l   as   ere   all but on   e   o us remain alive

A   l   as   here s all but one hun   o us ma n   live

A   lo   there   t one   o   em   ali

        on   all but one   main   l ie

A   long   li e

                        one   o us

A long   live

A long   er   one   o us   live

As long as   one   o us re   a   l

As long as   a   s   em in alive

152

Joanna Clarke

Once, The Kitchen was the Biggest Room in the House

People seem a little confused these days about what 'natural food' actually is. To look at the shelves in most health-food shops, you would conclude that 'natural food' is dried up stuff in bags and pills in jars. But let us use some common sense here.

Beyond the Concrete

Natural food comes from plants which have been grown in the same environment as yourself and are part of your personal ecosystem: that way, they are in harmony with the same laws and cycles of nature which are governing your own physiology; that way, also, your food has the natural ability to redress any imbalancing stresses in your body and will prevent disease. This is why natural food is healthy. Food from an alien environment will keep you alive but will not keep you in perfect health.

As you gaze out upon the asphalt and concrete which may well surround your home, the prospect of having to survive on meals grown in your own environment could be daunting.

Look beyond the concrete. We are rapidly losing them now, but, until modern obsession with size and uniformity in our vegetables took hold, Scottish land produced a wealth of different kinds of oats, peas and barley, potatoes and neeps, kale and leeks; all bred for their taste and texture. No need to go south for fruit: an abundance of berries thrived out there which were second-to-none. We still have a few of our dairy delicacies, our heather honey, Scotch beef, mutton and chicken. The hearty broths and spicy puddings traditional and natural to Scotland are what our bodies often need to maintain our health in this cool and damp climate with its long winter nights. Central heating and lights which replace daylight at the flick of a switch have not removed that need.

Farming with Gunpowder

I'm sure to hear a sceptical voice at this point telling me that there is no such thing as natural food unless we go out and grovel for roots and berries in the forest. The reason given for this claim is that farming itself is unnatural and that every plant and animal farmed has been so genetically altered by long-term breeding that they barely resemble their ancestors. I beg to differ: adapting your environment (including your food) to suit your own needs couldn't be more natural. This is progress. The outcome of progress is that the fruits of your life's work are passed on for the benefit of your children and grand-children.

Propagating plants to enhance whatever qualities in them you have found to be beneficial to yourself is simply working with nature. The modern trend for sowing millions of acres of near-identical plants in chemical-spiked soil is, in contrast, a fight with nature. Our twentieth century drive to mechanise agriculture has scaled up crop production to the point where we have replaced our health-promoting foods with disease-prone plants and monoculture malnutrition in ourselves. For us Scots, local monocultures are few and far between, but we have dismissed the crops of our heritage and made the imports from far off lands our staple diet.

And of course, using explosives to fire non-living DNA copied from other life-forms into your food is the ultimate departure from nature. The crops resulting from this assault will never have a natural environment to fit into anywhere and cannot nourish your physiology, nor strengthen you against illness.

Natural Food Processing

What we do with our food after it has grown is to process it to suit our needs. Food processing is natural and necessary. Typically, the lady of the house will select the food she wants according to its appearance, aroma and texture. She will clean it and discard unwanted parts before cooking it, fast or slow, according to its needs. The food is flavoured with herbs or spices and moistened with oil or cream. The dish is carefully stirred or mashed to disperse and amalgamate the ingredients. The result of natural food processing is that raw food materials are rendered digestible and nutritious, and the aim of it is to preserve the health of her family.

Processing with Es

Food processing can also be carried out using machines and chemicals. This can begin even before the food is grown when herbicides are applied to prepare the soil and is continued by the spraying of insecticides and fungicides during crop growth and again during storage. Typically, the food is taken into a factory where it (plus its pesticide load) is fed into a machine. The machine will likely reduce it to small pieces for more rapid exposure to the subsequent processing (time costs money) and will cook it for a minimum time (heat costs money). Then comes an army of Es: chemicals to stick it together or to break it up; chemicals to increase the final volume by thickening it, holding in air, or binding water; chemicals to reduce the need to heat it (heat costs money); chemicals to keep it 'fresh'; and finally more chemicals to replace the colour lost, to reinstate the vanished flavour and to add in vitamins which will look good on the label. What emerges from the machine is wrapped in plastic and a nice box and may be transported half-way across the globe. The result of chemical food processing is that the raw material is changed to a form which your body can barely recognise as food, and the aim of it is to make money for the manufacturer.

You are what you eat: the strange concoction in plastic from another part of the world becomes you. Is it any wonder that chronic diseases have increased exponentially in the 50 years since we began processing our foods with Es?

Foods which Process Themselves

We have gone one better now than just machinery and chemicals to process our food. We are manufacturing plants which process themselves. With a little chopping and changing of genes in a laboratory come tomatoes which thicken themselves, strawberries which sweeten themselves, self-vitaminising rice and pestilent maize. The future will logically hold cows genetically engineered with seaweed genes to make self-stabilizing whipped cream.

You are what you eat. Genetically modified foods have a warped vitality and a distorted physiology which will become you. They have the potential to unbalance any aspect of your physiology, and the potential to create chronic disease in one hundred percent of the population from birth to an early death.

We are already getting it wrong. Like most developed countries, Scotland has regressed from being a country of diverse and wholesome foods to one with a famine of plenty. Our health record is particularly bad. Poor health is a predictable symptom of a nation out of touch with the natural law of its land. The answer lies in eating more food from our own climate and less from the much warmer regions abroad. We have the technology now to make outstanding progress in the areas of agriculture and diet but are wasting precious resources fighting nature with chemicals and genes. The first step to perfect nutrition and perfect health is that we recognise what our 'natural food' really is.

Dee Rimbaud

From the Wondrous Burgh Of Eden Another Angel Falls

Ether sky on Crammond Promenade/ sun sinking into cold darkness/ oil black firth/ carious mouth/ its halitious breath stinging the eyes.

Tiredness in bones & head. The raw, filthy tiredness of chemical entropy. And the dreams & visions are far away. Over the hills and faraway. This. This. And that. Cauterised hopes. Pissing on cathartic fire. Cramped viscera. Ureic secretion. Dyscentric megababble. A toppled tower. A burnt library. A pile of words. This high. This. This. This & that. Sun sinking beyond dear green place. Saturated silhouette. Irreverent reverie. Penumbraic memorababble. A severing of tongues: dissection of brains. A hundred tribes trampling down the green grass. Shards. Slivers. The shattering of the glorified glass cow. The almighty lord, well displeased. The residents, diseased. A thousand plagues upon their heads. A thousand curses on the turncoat renegade.

Tap once, tap twice. There's no place like home

Acid tripping thru' Pilton Paradise. Skyscrapers scraping fibres of skin from the sky. Track marks down gangrenous veins . Empty Eldorado. Thunderbirds are go. The tough get going. Junked out on the briny Forth. Vultures circling high above, cutting arcs of stark black rainbow. Unclean rain silting up the river. The river running past Eve & Adam. A river of melted black macadam.

Shock sore eyes. Dirty dishes piled high. This high. In my sink of damaged dreams. Twenty dead salmon in rich deep crimson blood, thrashing angrily in stainless steel captivity: staring with accusing eyes.

This fish never swam. This tree never grew. This bell never rang. This puir wee chookie bird never flew,

The water washes over. Saline detergent. I emerge, less than clean. Sun sinks down,red & blistered, west of destiny. Beyond the queen's ferry. Vagina rex. God save her. And on, on into the sallow, slipping, listless, lapping, unfrothed waters. Spume spewing from unfine oil refineries.

I dip my spent wick. This. That. This & that. This clock goes 'tic toc'. The sun unwinds, turns back, turns black; and another angel falls.

A Beautiful Chemistry

One hundred and twenty beats to the minute and accelerating/ until deceived by the illusion of stillness/ chemical simulation of nirvana/ a foretaste of paradise to come/ ignoring the aftertaste and the cramps in yr guts/ dance entranced to strobed centre of the universe/ love everyone/ cry out/ inarticulate in yr ecstasy/ *this is awesome, ah fuckin love you man*/ the left field is always greener/ always/ and whatever you do dinnae chew gum/ coz you'll be grinding away like a fucking madman/ n'yer gob'll be totally fucked the morra/ and make sure you drink plenty of water. *See? Even in the beyond there are rules.*

First there is the anticipation/ then the rush/ it's like being sucked into paradise on the tail of a comet/ yr hot/ and when she touches you every pore of you orgasms forever/ and you're lost in her eyes/ a galaxy in her eyes/ spangles and an infinity of empty, dark space/ and you know now, the meaning of love/ the meaning of life/ falling into her eyes/ throbbing cascade/ into the heart of never never/ giving birth endlessly to each other/ grinning till you feel like yr head's going to split open/ *this is fuckin awesome man, ah love you/* what I mean to say is.../ poetry defeats me/ love defeats me/ life defeats me/ I submit/ and in submission, I am bliss.

And the beauty of this chemistry is the fragile empty hangover of a hundred morning afters/ the exquisite pain of having suffered to much love.

Rose Thou Art Ecstatic

She sinks down under the weight of stolen kisses,
Her wings a petrol spectrum of helplessness,
Flustering in the furious wind of gravity's angel.

Icon for our times, this ruby crow descending,
Spirit of a tarnished, deconstructed Christ,
All goodness wiped from her lips
In the rub of vinegar rags.

Purblind, a cascade of platitudes, a parachute
Of the emperor's finest silk: she crash lands,
Junked out on chemistry, crater-eyed and oblivious.

Dream Eclipses Reality

Yesterday I painted
Great big happy faces
On all the skyscrapers
In the Gorbals…
And what if skyscrapers
Really did scrape
The sky?
I would attach paintbrushes
Dripping with rainbow colours
To their radio masts
And lightning conductors.

VIR*tu*AL VIR*u*S

HELLo, I aM A gHOST in thE *mac*HIne
an ephemeral wIMPering WHISPer,
i AM not *HERe* or tHEre OR
in the tele*phone wiring,*
iT is NOT a cock *up*
at admi*n or*
a fauLT
iN
thE
SYstem
UnderP*INNIN*G
the sweet DReaMs
of your techNO*logical* u*top*ia……YeS?

Bill Williams

New Labour – New Nausea

When the call came to contribute to this collection the air waves were still reverberating from the stirring message delivered at Blackpool by Millennium Mandelson. Modernise or die was the gist of it.

Being in government does bring out the very worst in some people. The dying Tories were an instant turn-off almost to a man. When Home Secretary Howard took to the air it was a challenge to hit the off button before he could utter a single word.

Peter Mandelson is going the same way. But why is it that New Labour is quite so irritating? Is it the Armani suits and the rocket salad, is it cuddling up to pop stars or flaunting a tacky sponsorship deal from, of all people, a supermarket chain?

There was certainly a lot about old Labour that needed changing. Permanent Labour rule in the West of Scotland had led, it cannot be denied, to what was almost a contempt for the public. It almost seemed that the ruling classes were happy to keep their client people corralled in their Drumchapels and their Easterhouses, confident in the knowledge that their vote could always be wheeled out and the punters would never get ideas above their station.

There were cabals and cliques. Open government was not exactly a burning issue in the smoke filled rooms.

But that never was the whole story. Old Labour also had and has many very solid virtues. And it is the seeming denigration of these values that really lies at the heart of much of the unease over New Labour.

Given their emphatic Commons majority and the apparently interminable toils of the Opposition, one is bound to ask why the Government have to indulge in such economic machismo as they regularly do. At times it seems as though they really are bidding to out-Tory the Tories.

What else could explain even flirting with the idea of privatising the Post Office? Our nationally owned Post Office is one of the most efficient in the world. It turns in substantial profits, not for some murky

160

offshore corporation in some distant clime, but for our own national coffers. Even the Tories recognised that the public had no stomach at all for a privatised mail service. So why do New Labour even contemplate it?

The situation with the railways is even worse. Virtually the whole media agreed at the time that the Tory sell-off of our national rail system was a total disgrace. There were even prominent Tories who warned that catastrophe was looming. In the predictable shambles that have ensued what is New Labour doing about it? Much wringing of hands and an abject and humiliating retreat from the stated promise to take the railways back into national control.

It is almost as though some perverse pleasure was gained from denigrating decent Socialist policies that even the harshest economic criteria can show to be in the true long term public interest.

Or take the private finance initiative, another device much loved by the Tories and now taken into the bosom of New Labour. Detailed research has shown that many of the supposed "savings" generated by this piece of financial sleight of hand are in fact illusory, or at best very short lived. Assets that seem to be provided "free" by business look on closer inspection as though they could turn out to be very expensive in the long run. Yet new Labour dare not even countenance this possibility for fear, it would seem, of being called old hat. Hence we have Mandelson's desperate exhortation to be modern at all costs.

Rather than all the sickening toadying to big business and the aping of the discredited Tories, Labour should sometimes have the courage to stand up for socialist ideas. Despite the rantings of the Murdoch press, some of these ideas actually work very well and some national assets really have to be in State control.

In the case of the railways a no-nonsense warning from Labour at the time of the Railtrack flotation would have ensured that only the most hardened speculators would have taken on the risk. The company could have been promptly taken back into public ownership without shelling out huge sums to the opportunists who bought up the company for a song.

The regulatory framework with the railways, as with other privatised utilities, has shown itself to be so puny as to be almost worthless.

This blind pursuit of market forces with little or no regulation from the top could very well lead us to a position of private monopoly with key

161

elements of our economy being controlled from outside this country. Already there are worrying signs of this in the power industry. The North of Scotland Hydro Electric board, from being an admirable and powerful agent for social good in the Highlands in the days of Labour giants like Tom Johnston, has become, as privatised Hydro Electric, another vehicle for financial speculation wherever and whenever that can be done.

To add insult to the memory of this once great Scottish institution, the modern day successor to the Hydro Board shows utter contempt for sustainable energy projects, going out of its way either to rubbish them or where possible to saddle them with inflated costs as their price for collaboration. What a far cry from the founding body which should have shone like a beacon of inspiration..

"Old Labour" – I prefer to think of it as True Labour – should come off the defensive. They should not be mesmerised by Mandelson's claptrap about the wired world of the future. Sure the internet is a very useful tool, but it is just that. Neither should they be silenced by the slickly presented sound bite and the managed news release. Behind the sharp suits and the trendy Nick Nairn menu's there are enduring values that must be spoken up for.

Nationally owned operations need not be an economic disaster. They can operate efficiently for the benefit of the whole of society, not just a magic circle of fat cats and shareholders, but that is a truth that New Labour would seem to prefer to be suppressed, along with much else that a Freedom of Information Act might have brought out into the open.

But then that is another story – and another set of broken promises?

Jeff Torrington

Go Down Laughing!

a chapter

Fade into the morose strains of a cello. Shot of coffin rocketing from cloud-trimmed sky.

Sepulchral voice: In the end all men come to dust.

Snappy American voice: That's right! But if they're wised-up on what's going down, they'll insist on Byootessa !

Yes, Byootessa Caskets – built to last a deathtime, and to be had in the shade of your choice. Remember ! Only Byootessas have the fabulous Silverised Wundakwilt. So, look for the Silver Lining, and go get Byootessa – the Casket of Celebrities!

Jingle: Byootessas never fade away –

Safe and snug till Judgement Day!

'Well,' I asked Herman Eppledinker, whom I call Epple for short, 'what d'you think?'

'Don't see no Wundakwilt,' he said, as he peered into one of the ten thousand plastic coffins stacked around us. 'Jest empty in there.'

'Let me know if you happen on a full one,' I quipped, then – raising the lid of one – did! But this was no stiffo; it sat up'nd rubbed its silvery whiskers. It wasn't a vampire either, for it took a lettuce sandwich from its backpocket and began to munch on it.

'Good day t'you,' it said, confirming that it was human. 'You don't want to be making a habit of it, y'know: disturbing folks kip – invading their privacy.'

'Sorry, I'd no idea...'

'Course you didn't. Mistake. Easy to make. Dark in here. But you'll know in future, eh? A cross chalked on the lid of a settle means it's taken. Stacks of empties about though – see the Swamp cowboy – he'll fix you up.'

'Who's he, then?'

'Caretaker. Reasonable, his terms are. Warm in the winter, cool in the summer, these boxes. Wouldn't be without one. Reckon I'll take it with me when I kicks the old bucket!'

He cackled hoarsely, disposed of the remainder of his sandwich, then slammed down the casket's lid. I raised it again. 'Where do I find the caretaker?'

'Purple job, top of this stow, mate.'

Another outburst of his cackling was cut short by Epple, who, banging down the lid, whipped out a screwdriver, and nailed the coffin shut.

We began to climb over dusty tiers of multi-coloured caskets from which faint snores and rustling noises could be heard. As Aunt Toby had mentioned in her will, these coffins had been stored inside a concrete Lancaster Bomber which lay on its belly in Witchlaw Marsh. Built on a truly monumental scale – many times greater than the original plane it had been modelled on, it was claimed that more concrete had gone into its construction than had been used for the Hoover Dam Project.

The immense concrete Lancaster had resulted from a cockamamie notion of my eccentric Uncle Hubert (Washington) Wells, who'd intended to use it as a decoy in order to lure Jerry planes into a wasteful expenditure of their bombloads. However, as it turned out, only one of the Luftwaffes's raiders had visited the fake Lancaster, scoring a direct hit on it with a large wooden bomb which, upon impact, had – to a rendition of 'Uber Alles' by the Dusseldorf Male Voice Choir – sprouted from its tail a Nazi banner with 'Bang! – Love, Fritz!' emblazoned on it.

The plastic coffins venture had proved to be mad Hubert's final business floperoo, for after its promotion campaign, he'd gotten himself mangled while test-driving a prototype version of his revolutionary four-stroke, turnip-powered sleet-plough.

Once we'd reached the top of the coffin stack, Epple, in his usual ill-mannered way, wrenched open the lid of a purple coffin. Inside, there was this scrunched-up little guy who was clutching an empty bourbon bottle. There were books, newspapers, Lottery tickets, porno mags, records, and video tapes in there with'm, too: obviously, it was his living room.

'He's a deader,' Epple said. I nodded, then respectfully replaced the lid. Epple was about to screw him down but I vetoed this, since it was unlikely that the Witchlaw morgue would have such a thing as a screwdriver. They'd just about everything else; blue video shows; a continuously opened canteen; Kareoke Nites; as well as Line Dancing each Saturday evening.

While we stood there, the lid of yet another nearby purple casket creaked open. From this box there stepped an old bod who toted a powerful flashlamp. He wore a guano-spattered plug hat, a trashed-out reefer jacket, and badly frayed denim pants, the legs of which were stuffed into a pair of leather cowboy boots. Each of these items of clobber, including his hands and face, were bedaubed with enough clay to suggest that God hadn't got started yet.

Catching both Epple and me in the beam of his flashlamp, he grumpily asked: 'Well, what'll it be – week or by the month? Sixty pence the week – two quid the month. A shake in the morning costs tenpence. You cooks your own chow and sanitises your settle at least once a week. No pets of any kind – specially not 'gators nor pythons. No ceegareets nor whusky, and definitely no wilda-wild wimmen!'

I grinned and shook my head. 'We haven't come here for lodgings. Old timer.'

'You hasn't? What, then?'

'I'm Harvard (Wyoming) Wells – the new owner. And, furthermore' – I raised the lid of the stiffo's casket – 'we got us a dead caretaker.'

'That aint no caretaker,' said the old guy, laying the lamp's beam on the deader's grizzled face. 'This here's Sid Kidd. Sid was a Road Dog. Died last night, Sidd Kidd did.'

'Have you reported it?'

'What for?

'They might want to do an autopsy on'm. See if he croaked natural like.'

'They don't come any more natural, fella. Sid here was a hunner'nd five last week.' He swung his lamp so that its light bedazzled Epple. 'And who or what might this weird looking critter be?' he asked.

'Herman Eppledinker. He's going to help me clear out these boxes.'

'Eppledinker?' the old guy mused. 'Say wasn't there an Eppledinker who wrote: "Trouble at the Lazy L" ?'

'How the Lazy L should I know? Look, Mister - ?'

'Shrootz. Solomon Shrootz. Pleased t' know ya.'

We locked mitts.

'Sure is an unusual place you've got here, Mr Shrootz'

'Durned if I see anything peculiar about it.'

The lamp beam danced along the Lancaster's awesome cathedral-like roof which was faintly freckled with low-wattage bulbs that cast a murky light upon the multi-coloured coffin stows which stood the entire length of the fuselage.

'Why don't you fellas step along to my office – it's up'n the cockpit.' said the Swamp Cowboy.

'Mr Shrootz,' I asked him as we threaded our way through a maze of coffin-stacks, 'what're you going to do about Old Sid?'

'Plant'm, I guess.'

'In Witchlaw Cemetery you mean?'

'No, in the marsh; settle down real quick they does.'

'You did say "they" Shrootz?'

He nodded 'This is where them Road Dogs come to hang up their boots, young fella.'

'It's all got to stop ,' I told him.

He canted his head. 'Sorry, Mister, don't quite catch your drift.'

I explained who I was and why I'd come.

'You means you're taking over the spread? New Boss of the Ranch, eh?'

I nodded. 'That's right, pardner. Soon truck convoys will come a-rolling to carry off these Resurrection Crates to the folks who need'm most.'

'Gittin' them rigs here aint gonna be all that easy,' Shrootz warned as he paused in the mid-upper gunner's section and peered out; joining him, I was just in time to see the Marsh Road disappearing.

'Durned funny Marsh,' Shrootz observed.

'You mean this happens often?'

'Regular as clockwork.'

'But when will the Road resurface?'

Shrootz humped his skinny shoulders. 'Can't rightly say – clockwork aint all that regular, is it?'

'Are you telling me we're stuck on this dammed stone kite until that blasted Road shows again?'

'There's a secret way out.'

I sighed. 'Now you're talking! Let's be having it, then.'

But Shrootz was shaking his head. 'Paper it was drawed on got took by a Road Dog. Had to clear'm out on account of him catching one of them defectious diseases. Road was down at the time, but he had to go just the same. Rules is rules, gotta enforce'm.'

'And did he go?'

'Yup – right to the bottom of the Marsh! I gave'm the escape route all right, but didn't the giddy old gopher go'n hold the map arsy-versy.'

'Surely you made a copy'

He nodded. 'It's in one of these here caskets.'

'But there're ten thousand of the damned things!'

'That aint exactly so, Mr Marshlord.' Shrootz plucked a notebook from his hip pocket and thumbed his way through its dog-eared pages. 'Cording to my last inventionary there's only 9,660 corpse cases left.'

'Where'd the rest of'm go?'

'Into the Marsh. Like I said, this is where them Road Dogs come to hang up their wanderin' boots.' He nodded. 'Gets the feeling in their bones, they does, and they knows it's time to climb on board Mad Hubert's Winged Folly and take off to Kingdom Come.'

Shrootz paused a moment to chuck a coffin hinge at a huge rat that was grooming itself on top of a stow of rainbow-coloured caskets.

'I expect the place is swarming with those plaguey pests,' I said.

'Not so's you'd notice,' replied Shrootz. 'Rats is fussy critters. They don't take to airyplanes, and that goes double for concrete non-flying jobs like this one.' Shrootz paused to drag clear the intricate lacework of a cobweb that festooned a pile of polkadot caskets.

'I see you're on the Internet,' I joked. 'Must be the most unique Web Site around, eh?' From his baffled look, it was obvious that Shrootz didn't know where I was coming from. Likewise, Epple, whose fizog wore its usual doltish expression which was concocted from a compound of jawdroop, trenched-brow, and lip-drool.

Faster than a chameleon's tongue, Shrootz's hand shot into the air and crushed a wasp in mid-flight. He wiped its pulped remains on the tail of his reefer jacket to which there clung the broken legs and snapped wings of previous kills.

Moving on, Shrootz returned to the subject of the road Dogs. 'Course, they don't all buy-the-farm. Nope, a week or so stretched out in one of these boxes is all some of 'em needs to git their juices all perked up again. So, stead of popping their clogs, they're reaching for their boots, and gittin' themselves ready to do some more Road Dogging.'

As we sneezed our way amongst the dusty piles of caskets, heading for the cockpit, we came across a weird-looking contraption. It seemed it was now my turn to be perplexed by alien technology. The gadget looked like a scaled-down model of the starscope they've got over at Jod Bank. But, the thing served a more down-to-earth function.

'It's a what?' I asked Shrootz

'Road-Dogapult' said the old gink laconically. 'So's I can spread them dead uns around the Marsh.'

'How's it work?' Epple asked.

Shrootz took up an empty coffin. 'You just plants this here box on them rollers, like so. Draws back on this here hydrobolic lever. Press this button, and – whoosh! – off she goes!'

Epple, who can be so aggravatingly sceptical at times – in fact, most of the time – was shaking his head. 'It's bound to fall off the ramp when loaded,' he predicted.

'Well, of all the disbelieving coyotes!' Shrootz looked really fizzed up. 'Maybe ifn I climbs in you'll accept it?'

Epple nodded. Shrootz clambered into the coffin and, as he'd forecast, the box stayed put on the Dogapult's ramp, until, that is, Epple thumbed the ejector button: one second the old geezer's lying there, arms crossed on his chest, eyelids clamped, the next, both he and the bye-bye box went shooting at an amazing velocity through an adjacent porthole.

'You oughtn'to have done that, Epple.'

'He'd no call to cousin me off on prairie trash like the coyote,' he grumbled. 'Speshly not them disbelieving kind.'

'C'mon,' I said, 'let's go hunt for that "escape-route". Don't want to be stuck here overnight. Your Ma'll be worried.'

He nodded. 'Rain caused it, I guess.'

'Caused what, Epple?'

'You know that railway embankment our shack's built on?'

I nodded.

'Well, last night it melted clean out from under us, and the shack kinda moved out onto the tracks.'

'Kinda?'

'Jest Ma's bedroom.'

'And what did your Ma have to say about that?'

'Nothing much – she's a real heavy sleeper.'

'Jumping Judas! Epple, there're trains hammering down that track every twenty minutes!'

He shook his head. 'Not today there aint.'

I dreaded to ask the next question: 'How come?'

'Remember the scrap metal I was telling you about – stuff I loaded on Dingofoot Donaghue?'

'Rails?' I said.

Epple nodded. 'That's right – rails.'

I shook my head. 'You worry me at times, Epple, you really do. C'mon, let's go hunt for that Marsh-Exit Map.'

It was of course the longest of long shots: looking for a scrap of paper in a concrete bomber that was tightly packed from props. to tailfin with multi-coloured coffin stacks (the wings, too, had been modified to accommodate even more caskets) just had to be an exercise in futility.

I finally came up with a notion that might help to lower the daunting odds a tad. Roughly, the ploy was this: I'd climb into a casket and sham being dead. Epple would waken all the road Dogs and tell'm I'd snuffed it from the dreaded Swamp Pox. This, I figured, would rouse such a panic in their ragged ranks that they'd begin a collective search for the escape map, thereby creating a situation of 'many hands make light work…'

At first all went fine. Epple flushed forty or so Dogs from their settles, and they all came to give me the onceover.

'Best screw'm down,' said one of them.

'Yeah, keep the Pox in its box,' agreed another Road Dog.

A winking Epple obliged with his screwdriver.

'Looks like the Swamp Cowboy's already vamoosed,' someone noted, then went on to propose that I should be ejected.

'You never can tell with that Swamp Pox,' he said, an observation that aroused a throaty rumble of assent from his fellow Road Dogs.

I sweated enough to kill off all known germs, and, probably, wiped out a billion or so of those swamp bugs as yet unclassified. But, to my astonishment, didn't the semi-moronic Epple come to my rescue when, against all odds, he managed to dissuade the Road Dogs from feeding me into the Dogapult by suggesting that it would be best to keep the deader on ice till the Witchlaw coroner had confirmed that it'd been the victim of Swamp Pox. But, right now, he told them, their priority was to locate the escape map, so that they could quit the Plane en masse until it'd been fumigated.

I lay there in the claustrophobic dark listening to the Road Dogs and Epple turning over the coffin stacks. After a while things got suspiciously quite. I yelled for Epple and, suprisingly, he came.

'What's going on?' I queried. 'Where are the Road Dogs?'

'In the Marsh,' he said

'You mean crossing it?'

'No, I means in it. Guess their leader was holding the map wrong way up.'

'C'mon, then,' I bawled, 'get me out of here!'

'Can't,' he replied, 'one of them Road Dogs pinched my screwdriver.'

'Find another!'

'I'll have to be going,' he said.

'Going? You mean you've got the map?'

'Road's up again. Be seeing you, Harv. Kinda worried about Ma...'

'Epple, open this bloody box at once! D'you hear?'

'Sure hope your Swamp Pox clears up,' he said, then he was off. I heard his footsteps pelting the length of the fuselage, then, after a considerable pause, the door that'd been improvised from the tail-gunner's aperture, closed with a distant slam. There's no way around it – Epple is definitely one square short of a chessboard! Frantically, I tried to claw my way from that Resurrection Crate. There's no need for lurid details – I was in, and I wanted OUT!

An idea suggested itself: if I managed to rock the coffin from its stow, maybe it would burst apart when impacted on the concrete floor.

Things didn't work out the way I'd envisaged. As I lay there in my pitch black, perfectly intact, plastic prison, lapping blood from my split lip, I heard a scratching noise on the casket's lid. Yippee! Rescue was at hand! Someone was unscrewing the box's brass nails. Moments later, I was unbunged. I came bounding from that box faster'n 'Tornado Tom', the greyhound champ of Gideon Dog Track could've trapped even with a fizzing stick of jelly tied to his tail. My rescuer was not Epple, as I had surmised, in fact, it turned out to be a sneezing Solomon Shrootz.

'Who in tarnations nailed you in there?' he asked after his nose had loosed off another round of sneezes. 'That maniac pardner of yours I'll bet.'

I asked him how he'd escaped from the Marsh.

'Got lucky is all – landed on a giant tussock of pepper-weed. Was stranded though till the Road came up' He plucked a small glossy green frog from his bird-spattered plug hat.

'Too bad about them Road Dogs – went lickety-splittin' into that swamp like they was a buncha lemons.'

' "Lemmings," you mean.'

'Same difference. Anyways, they came here to turn up their toes, didn't they?'

Squelchingly, Shrootz led me to the cockpit-cum-office which was screened-off with mosquito netting and illuminated by a hissing kerosene lamp that stood on the navigator's gigantic desk and was being continuously bombarded by squadrons of kamikaze moths.

Paperback Westerns cascaded from sagging overstuffed shelves and every ledge and lean-on accommodated cans of grub, although the bulk of it appeared to consist of the chow favoured by 'The Riders of the Purple Sage' and their prairie pals – chuck like canned pork and beans, bully beef and beans, bison's balls and beans, and, no doubt, if you looked hard enough, you'd find beans and beans.

'Swell Boss, yourn uncle. A touch loco, maybe, but when he took up on the hobo-herding biz he put me in charge of this here place so's he could git on with his invenshins and stuff. Always made sure I'd plenty to read, and that I didn't want for a platter of veetals.'

Shrootz began to kick his way through the empty chuck cans that cluttered the floor. A pair of mice who'd been night clubbing inside a near-empty can of syrupy peaches, came squeaking from it and disappeared into a crevice in the massive stone instrument panel. A bluebottle twanged past my ear. The place hummed like a stoker's armpits, which was yet another reason for me to resist his 'park yoself' invitation. 'Plague yourself !' was more likely.

'Say, where you off to, young fella?' Shrootz cried.

'Got loads to do,' I said, ripping aside the Velcroed mosquito netting. 'Be seeing you real soon, old timer…'

I sprinted blithely out onto the mud-clogged Marsh Road that curved comfortingly towards blessed Witchlaw. Shrootz waved to me from the Cockpit. I waved back. He waved once more. I reciprocated. Suddenly, there was no Road curving comfortingly anywhere!

'Shoulda mentioned,' said Shrootz after he'd eventually succeeded in lassoing me, 'that there Road always makes a point of going down at nine.'

'But it's only eight!'

He grinned. 'It don't take no reckoning of British Summer Time. By the way,' Shrootz drawled as I stood shivering by his peat-stove, ''cording to my 'rithmetic, I gotta an almighty slab of unpaid salary due.'

Aptly, at that very moment, a fat leech that'd been having itself a blood-banquet on my arm, unhitched its gore-pipe and dropped clear.

'Yeah, yeah,' I said, as the swamp Cowboy sought to justify his back-wages claim. 'Work it out'n caskets. And take your cut...'

But Shrootz wasn't listening: he was reading a Western called "Trouble At The Lazy L" by Leatherstud Eppledinker.

Freddy Anderson

Never No More!
(To the tune of 'The Wild Rover)

When I was a young man
I used to have a dream
That voting for Labour
Was my duty supreme:
But my eyes have been opened,
No longer I'm gulled-
A vote for New Labour
Is a vote for John Bull.

Chorus

Oh no nay never, never no more
Will I vote for New Labour,
No nay never no more.

I went into an alehouse
I used to frequent
And on a few drams
My pittance was spent
I asked for the slate then
The landlord said 'Nay,
For clients like you, sir,
I can have every day.

Chorus

Like a Tory, Blair's cheating
Poor folk on the dole,
And single parent mothers
He drives up the pole:
He bribes the rich bosses,
Loves Thatcher as well,
I wish all these twisters
Were scorching in hell.

Oh no nay never, never no more
Will I vote for New Labour,
No nay never no more.

No more waste your vote, man,
On twisters like Blair
Who line their own pockets
And cut your welfare:
If you are true Scottish
Take counsel from me
Stand up for your country
And vote SNP

Oh no nay never, never no more
Will I vote for New Labour
No nay never no more.

Richard Demarco

The Artist as Explorer

The relationship of Edinburgh Arts, a 7,500 mile journey into the origins of European culture, to the developing contemporary Art language of the twentieth century.

Extended from a paper presented to the University of Toronto's Symposium on the "Celtic Consciousness". 5-12 February 1978.

Introduction

I wrote this 20 years ago in the eighth year of my collaboration with Joseph Beuys when I was asked by him to work with The Special Unit of HM Prison Barlinnie as personified by the artistic achievements of Jimmy Boyle and Larry Winters. Joseph Beuys was a politician, economist, philosopher, teacher, biologist, artist and social reformer. He was inspired by the work of The Unit and questioned deeply the reasons for Jimmy Boyle being transferred from The Unit back into the normal Scottish prison system as defined by HMP Saughton.

Joseph Beuys sued the Secretary of State's office saying that Jimmy Boyle should not be transferred from the Special Unit and had earned the right to call himself a free citizen by becoming an artist in prison. The court case was to no avail. Joseph Beuys lost legally but gained a moral victory. The Demarco Gallery, however, suffered grievously by the fact that the Scottish Arts Council thought fit to remove its entire financial support. As a result of the exhibition at the 1980 Edinburgh Festival which Beuys dedicated to Jimmy Boyle and The Special Unit, Beuys made two blackboards entitled "Johnny Boyle Days" which were sold to the Statisches Museum, Moenchengladbach. Beuys donated £16,000 from such sales to the Demarco Gallery proving his point that "kunst = kapital", "art = wealth." He was emphasising the fact that the artist personifies "wealth" and "health" in society. It was an exercise in what Beuys called "social sculpture."

Joseph Beuys loved Scotland. He visited it eight times between 1970 and 1982. He concentrated great efforts on the Celtic culture of Europe, believing that his cultural origins were Celtic. He was born in Kleve, in a Celtic and therefore Roman Catholic enclave on the banks of the Rhine where the ancient Celts had established settlements as missionaries bringing Christianity from Scotland and Ireland into the heartland of Europe. He worked incessantly from 1970 to 1982 in both Scotland and Ireland inspired by this vision of Celtic Europe. He was undoubtedly the first artist of the 20th century with a firm conviction that the role of the artist was to question deeply all political and economic systems. He loved the Celtic imagination; he wanted to establish his concept of a Free International University in Ireland; he worked hard to build bridges between the Protestant and Catholic factions in Northern Ireland.

Eventually he was inspired by his experience of the Giant's Causeway and his love of nature, expressed in his deep respect for the oak tree as King of the Forest, to create a sculpture consisting of 7,000 oak trees planted in juxtaposition with 7,000 basalt stones. This sculpture, begun in the late 20th century, would come to full maturity half way through the third millennium. The basalt stones represented nature over a period of time, over millions of years, reaching back into the origins of the earth. The oak tree venerated by the Druids and by the early Christians represented man living in harmony with nature. This majestic work entitled simply "7,000 Eichen" is as much a political statement for the people of Kassel as it is a work of art, built into the very centre of the city, into its main thoroughfares and parks, involving every aspect of the city's public services in the initial process of installation over a period of three years. Joseph Beuys raised the money largely through selling other art works valuing millions of pounds. In this way it was a gesture of love for his fellow human beings and an act of faith in the future of mankind.

Joseph Beuys believed that making art was part of a healing process, putting right the wrongs inflicted by human beings upon themselves and upon the planet. He died in his mid-sixties firmly convinced that the role of the artist was yet to be understood and utilised. The artist's work is not identified with the worlds of tourism and leisure, for him the artist was at the forefront of the battle that must be waged daily to defend the freedom of the individual and the principles of justice within a post-second world war society.

He was a European through and through, he loved all of Europe and in the midst of the period of Martial Law in Poland he drove a truck containing 650 of his artworks and 20 cases of good German wine as a gift to the people of Poland. This collection is now in the Lodz Museum of Art. The wine was enjoyed by the artist and friends of the \museum. Beuys chose afterwards as his statement of love for Poland to spend afterwards some days in the Masurian Lakes. His whole life and work dignifies the very meaning of the word 'art'. It is sad that there are very few of his major works in Scotland, but I am hoping that when the Scottish National Gallery of Modern Art opens its new extension it will exhibit the works of Joseph Beuys which he donated to the Demarco Gallery, and that these works can be seen alongside the large and significant archive which documents his commitment to Scotland and his collaboration with Scottish artists, gallery directors, politicians, scientists, students, teachers, businessmen and arts administrators.

Among my clearest memories of him is his contribution to the conference entitled *"The Black and White Oil Show"* which involved him in a three hour lecture following the three hour lecture by Buckminster Fuller. This took place in a building he liked to call the "Poorhouse" in the Foresthill area of Edinburgh. He spent the whole day engaged passionately in debate with representatives of the oil industry, when, in 1974 at the Edinburgh Festival, the North Sea Oil Industry was in its infancy. He questioned the nature of wealth in the form of black gold. He did not think too highly of the giant oil platforms as symbols of Scotland. Standing in front of Greyfriars Bobby's statue, near to the "Poorhouse", he pointed to a headline in the Daily Mirror showing a picture of the oil platform with the words "first of the giants" and held it up against the image of Greyfriars Bobby suggesting that when North Sea oil was regarded as a short-lived phenomenon the image of the little Scotch Terrier would survive as a giant figure representing its capacity to remain faithful to its human master in life and beyond the grave.

I loved his sense of the ironic and his playful humour, he was a consummate politician and those who believe in the future of Scotland with its own Parliament would do well to honour the memory of Beuys as a great European who loved Scotland and the capacity of its people to contribute more than their fare share to the general treasurehouse of Europe.

Joseph Beuys and the Celtic Kinloch Rannoch Symphony

Joseph Beuys had a great influence on my work as a Gallery Director. He has played the role of mentor through his own need to rediscover the

Celtic origin of Europe. He taught me an unforgettable lesson with his fifty-six hour long art work called "Celtic Kinloch Rannoch –The Scottish Symphony". It was sculpture, as well as music, painting, and art in progress. It was an art lesson par excellence and it recalled long-forgotten Celtic rituals. Joseph Beuys was then regarded as "Avant-Gardist" but this work reassured me that indeed he is a traditionalist perfecting and understanding the countless generations of Artists' spirits who touch upon his own spirit. The work was a kind or requiem, hinting at the ritual of the Catholic Mass, praising the still effective and living reality of the artists Joseph Beuys needs and admires to extend his own art. There was a long list of artists' names on a tiny sheet of paper pinned on one of the walls of the Edinburgh Art College life-room where the whole event was enacted. The list was indeed in the form of a cryptic question "Where are the souls of Van Gogh, Duchamp, Piero della Francesca, William Nicholson, Fra Angelico" etc., and it ended with "… and Leonardo da Vinci?", who is perhaps the artist nearest to the image I have of Joseph Beuys. The whole room reverberated with the sound of long-forgotten European cultures linked to the voices of these artists. It was a sounding board for the past, present and future of art activity. It was a traumatic experience. It involved me for eight hours a day, for a week. It rid me of all the dead wood that I had been, until then, reluctant to cut away from the structure I had built in the name of the Demarco Gallery. A new gallery had to be created to deal with an artist such as Joseph Beuys – the embodiment in this one art work of the composer, dancer, musician, sculptor, painter, teacher and priest. He told me that the ordinary white cube space of the gallery's exhibition rooms was inadequate. That art could only be about work being done in a room where the evidence of physical labour, of those who have previously worked there, is not yet eradicated. Joseph Beuys added his marks to the countless marks of oil-paints and brushes which bespattered the life-room floor and walls – the evidence of work by past generations of students, including myself. Joseph Beuys used the whole room, he used the walls, covering them with globules of gelatine. He used the corners, blocking them off and protecting them with wooden boards, thus suggesting they were not just about angles but angels too – they were key points holding the mystery of the room as work-space together.

He used a grand piano, six tape recorders, two portable tape recorders, two film projectors and a black board, electric cables, two long planks of wood, a metal tray, two milk bottles, a walking stick and his own presence in collaboration with the Danish sculptor-composer Henning Christiansen to persuade me that the experience of art does not necessarily happen in a neat and tidy fashion as a framed art object within the walls of a Bond Street-style art gallery.

So the Demarco Gallery learned to adapt itself, to accommodate the space needed by Joseph Beuys and all the other Artists who made "Strategy-Get Arts" a turning point in the development of 20th century art.

Edinburgh Arts – a 7,500 mile journey inteo The Expanded Present, a search for Pre-Renaissance European peripheral cultures particularly that of the Celt

The art of Joseph Beuys makes thought manifest, representing action and the need to explore the space beyond the art world. "Edinburgh Arts" is not the best name for the experiment which is intended to extend the normal activities of a contemporary art gallery operating within a part of Europe strongly associated with the Celtic world.

This age of ours is short on action and overloaded with planning and theorising. It is important to wed thought to action, the imagination to physical experience. Even as I write I know any written words are only valid as a small part of a living experiment – an ongoing course of action.

I am reassured by the interest among artists in the concept of a Journey as defined by "Edinburgh Arts". Their attitude could be best summed up by that of the American art critic Jack Burnham, who has for years been interested in the occult in relation to contemporary art, particularly in the work of Duchamp. In a letter to me he described his own personal interest in the 1977 version of the Edinburgh Arts Journey. "Partially, my interest in the Celtic journey is concerned with pre-Christian religion and the obvious presence of a female godhead which, in a sense, is the unknowable, the "Holy Ghost" which plays such a key role but obscure part in Christian texts and liturgy. It seems apparent to me that a "male" godhead presupposes an illusionary temporary cycle (e.g. 'history') which decays in terms of its adherence to natural or sacred time cycles; it is essentially mechanical, subject to the forces of friction and gravity, and hence prone to decay. Art History as we know it through the Christian-Judaic traditions, is the study of these shifting standards and aesthetics. I assume my interest in the megalithic sites of Great Britain and Europe is to find and experience the architectonic female counterpart of our "Father Time". In other words, my interests are more aesthetic and intuitive than scholarly. "Roots" are a big business these days."

The essential nature of Edinburgh Arts lies in the fact that it is about taking action. It is a journey, the extension of that journey which began in 1972 with the first Edinburgh Arts project. It has always been an attempt to introduce artists to the energy of places, both historic and prehistoric, which reveal the creative nature of mankind to a degree little known in our world of contemporary art. Nowadays the spirit of art is overwhelmed by the spirit of technology. The imbalance has gradually worsened since the Renaissance failed to see the Dark Ages as full of that light which only art can reveal. The 20th century artist can all too easily be defined and encapsulated within the majority of essentially static institutions in the form of art galleries, schools, fairs, biennales, where a mindless belief in the inevitability of progress can be encouraged by the view of history as a linear structure.

Edinburgh Arts is a state of flux, not a static situation; physical action not theory. As a journey, it attempts to provide a dynamic link between centres which are too easily ignored by the contemporary art world, centres where the spirits of art and technology are enduringly balanced in the form of megalithic circles and burial mounds, sacred wells, pools and springs, ancient tracks and crossroads, monasteries, parish churches with their graveyards, and the secret places found high on hill and mountain tops and islands which resist, by their isolation, the improving hand of the modern guardian. There are, as well, the places of habitation and work of those contemporary artists whose working habits and environments communicate their at-oneness with the physical world. It includes, too, those places usually defined by small communities where human beings work with dignity and, through their daily tasks, communicate unselfconsciously in what is tantamount to a timeless art language linked powerfully to a specific geographic location. I think not only of the bell-ringers of Youlgreave, the lace-makers of Gozo, the fishermen of Sligo, but also of the officers and prisoners of the Special Unit of HM Prison, Barlinnie.

Normally a prison is low in spiritual energy and represents the very opposite space to that of a journey, and that of course is its essential weakness. It works against the full experience of the world, the life-giving feel of the out-of-doors, the ebb and flow of natural phenomena; of wind and weather, time and tide, and the normal forms of human communication through the family structure and the normal dialogue between the male and female roles in any community. Neither does the prison offer the risk or challenge inherent in the journey which would search out these experiences.

The Edinburgh Arts Journey is therefore unthinkable if it does not take into account the obscenity of man-made corrective systems which do not allow for regeneration. The mind or spirit cannot become or remain healthy if it endures a prolong assault from an unnatural environment. The journey is therefore a life-line to and from the prison. Fortunately the Scottish Prison Service has produced a life-enhancing point of contact to which the Edinburgh Arts Journey could be connected. It is the Special Unit which is a community of sixteen prison officers and four prisoners who together wish to create an alternative within the Scottish Prison Service to a system which has, for too long, been obliged to curb violent protest from prisoners with more violence. It is a courageous experiment, in its fourth year of perilous existence. It somehow survives in a daily struggle against long-established attitudes within the Prison Service which resist the forces of change and risk. All major decisions regarding its development are made by all the members of the community by group meetings. All the prisoners are serving either life or long term imprisonment and have been considered beyond the control of normal prison methods.

The Unit has already produced two outstanding creative souls who have been discovered and supported by the community itself to work as artists. One of them, Larry Winters, recently died tragically, but his poetry and courageous support of the Unit's life continues to be a positive force for good within the Unit. His poem "Yer Bloody Society" is a warning to all those who are not on guard against the negative forces at work within our society.

> "Hear the blind man as he sings
> For pennies

Hear the crying of children as
They die of hunger
See the smoke from the burning
Of wheatgrain
Hear the slow sign of sadness it
Groans for the lonely
See the flames from the bombs no
Warning is given
Taste the fumes of poison we daily
Are breathing
Feel something as children
Are murdered
Think daily of what you are doing
To prevent it
And try only try

Tho' your knees are atremble
To stop the machine that is killing
Your mother
The Earth
And her children"

Thankfully his friend Jimmy Boyle continues his work as a sculptor and writer expressing a strong commitment to the Unit and his hopes for a change in the official government attitudes towards the basic human rights of prisoners coping with conditions which inflict sensory deprivation on both prison officers and prisoners alike. Jimmy Boyle is the product of the urban jungle of Glasgow's Gorbals slum. His temperament is that of the Celt. From a life of terrifying violence he has accepted the role of peacemaker between criminal elements we reject and the law enforcers set up to protect society from its own self-centred weakness. He is the living proof that we all can be reborn, even the most violent and destructive of us, to a creative life. His life's work is now the Unit. Every effort of his life as an artist helps bring the Unit and with it the Prison Service into a dialogue with artists. His dialogue with Joseph Beuys has been especially fruitful.

He well understands the Edinburgh Arts Journey as a necessary extension of the space defined by the Unit wherein the human spirit can be reassured and strengthened by a poetic vision of life. Jimmy Boyle's role in the Unit continues the work of Lugus, the maker of art objects, containing the spiritual elements which all communities have to utilise. Jimmy Boyle has been on the journey since 1974. He has not yet been allowed to participate outside the prison walls in a physical sense, although he has helped many Edinburgh Arts participants to remain loyal to the journey, and not to take for granted their freedom to participate physically. He knows well the need to face the dangers of the journey even as it is defined within the confines of the Unit. He knows the journey's space is as hard to deal with as the precipitous slopes the mountaineer negotiates en route to the mountain top. He sees the need to incorporate the Unit's restricted dimensions into the limitless dimensions of the journey.

The Edinburgh Arts Journey is A Reconnaisance

Most journeys in this world, polluted by ill-conceived tourists, are advertised as short and comfortable. The Edinburgh Arts Journey is long and arduous. It is the very opposite experience to that which the modern traveller would seek. It offers no place of rest. It does not linger in the beautiful environments which would tempt participants to forget their loyalty to the journey itself. The journey provides an uncharted landscape for those who have the instincts and attributes of explorers, of those who, like transatlantic yachtsmen, know that a weather eye must be kept constantly on the elemental forces which form the journey's physical reality. They have to be prepared to live and work in a constantly moving community for days on end, sharing and contributing to one and the same forward-looking, ever changing experience. They must know, as does the relay race runner, that carrying the baton which represents the whole journey even for a short time can make the difference between success or failure, not just for oneself but for others. A state of timelessness can be achieved by the very spiral form of the journey, and by the awareness of places which resist definition by rational thought. At the very beginning and at the ending there is the reality of the Special Unit at Barlinnie, with its own consciousness of time and space so unrelated to that offered by contemporary art galleries. So the aim of the journey is simply the journey, no matter how long anyone participates. The only entry into the journey is by means of travelling intensively to a degree that alters the awareness of each participant. It deliberately causes a shift of gear. It does not guarantee anyone anything, but even those participants who joined the 1977 journey only for a day or two sensed the implications involved, and received something they considered valuable. Doing part of it, they contributed to the energy. They ceased to intellectualise about it. They began to understand the journey as a relentless physical reality. Whatever happened was fortuitous, allowed to be found, allowed to happen in the ideas generated, in the dialogues and friendships developed among the participants, and between the participants and those met with on the journey – people such as the art collector Tom Alexander and his friend Robert McLellan, playwright and writer of the official guide to the Isle of Arran, Jack Price, the innkeeper and guardian of Dartmoor's Fingle Bridge, and Wiliam Shimwell, the village schoolmaster of Youlgreave, as well as artists in their studios – Margo Sandeman, David and Claire Nash, Peter Blake, Jann Haworth, Patrick Heron, Victor and Wendy Pasmore and art patrons such as Count Giuseppi Panza di Biumo. There were gallery directors in their galleries, such as Alberto Moretti in Florence, Massino Valsecchi in Milan – and those who have created their own highly personal centres of creativity – Gabriella Cardazzo in Somerset, Paul and Penny Burns in Dorset, not obviously structured as art galleries – Li Yuan Chia in Cumbria, Marie Claridge in Gozo. All of them are extending the journey by the rhythm and pattern of their own lives. Their lives are interwoven with the lives of those Edinburgh Arts travellers who learned that each day provides the experience of a small journey within a larger one.

Brian Quail

Trident – Blair's Blame, Scotland's Shame

I am writing this crouched in a leaky tent, pitched on a Somme type morass of squelching mud and rotten vegetation, against a background of incessant rain and yet more rain. Black beetles scurry guiltily from under boxes and blankets, and contend with earwigs for lebensraum. The midges have given up, or been drowned – the only compensation for the relentless rain.

This is indeed a battle front; the scene of a crucial yet completely non-violent (on one side at least) conflict. I am in a field near Coulport, some 40 miles from Glasgow. Yesterday I watched as the enemy sailed past – an immense grey evil Leviathan sliding down Loch Long, escorted by tugs and police launches. This was HMS Vanguard, the first of Britain's Trident submarines, now joined by three others and awaiting a final fourth, the grotesquely named HMS Vengeance. Each single nuclear submarine carries 48 nuclear warheads, and each warhead is 8 times more powerful than the bomb that destroyed Hiroshima, where the final death toll was 200,000. This means that each submarine is specially designed to slaughter around 77 *million* people. A truly horrendous British achievement – the world's most powerful machine for the mass incineration of human being, the ultimate in mechanised mass-murder.

This is one side of the battlelines. Against this unimaginable destructive power are gathered the forces of peace, the Trident Ploughshares 2000 activists. There are more than 100 of us here; all of us have undergone training in non-violence and are committed to freeing Britain and the world from Trident by the year 2000. We are pledged to openly, democratically, non-violently and accountably disable Britain's criminal and illegal weapon of mass destruction, the Trident nuclear missile system. Our actions are based on well-established legal and moral principles. War crimes are not committed by states, they are committed by individuals, and it is the individual's duty to uphold the law.

There are people from more than a dozen nationalities here, people of all types and ages. A Lutheran priest from Sweden, a student from Tokyo, experienced veterans from Greenham Common, environmentalists from Australia, folk from Faslane Peace Camp. Young and old, all are united in their belief in peace and non-violence.

We are taking action because it is our duty and right to oppose state plans for genocidal war. As Richard Falk, the Professor of International Law in Princeton USA said: *"Everyone has the right and duty to say NO to illegal State Policy...It is not disobedience but the enforcement of the law to refuse to be an accomplice to the preparation of nuclear war".* Which – I think – says it all.

These were the notes I made at the start of our camp, on August 11th. Since then, after an initial week of relentless rain, followed by some beautiful sunny weather, our spirits and our inner strength have grown considerably. People have found in each other the mutual power and inspiration to face the ultimate evil, the nuclear death machine. The setting up of the Ploughshares camp at Coulport has drawn extensive coverage from the foreign media. There was a front-page story in the Guardian magazine of August 26th.

Paradoxically, the Scottish media have virtually ignored our action. As if it were a matter of no consequence that 120 people from a dozen different nations should come together in Scotland to confront Britain's submarine superbelsen, and to endure no less than 114 arrests. I cannot explain this silence; I only know that it is inexcusable.

Because all British nuclear bombs are now stored here in Scotland, and all Britain's nuclear submarines sail out on patrol from Scottish waters, I believe there is a very real and profound moral obligation on the people of this country to raise their voices loud and clear, to tell the government that we will not tolerate this conspiracy to commit war crimes being conducted in our land and against our wishes.

Trident is as undemocratic as it is immoral. Repeatedly polls show that some 80% of Scots do not want it. The churches have condemned Trident; the Scottish Labour Party and SNP reject it. Leaders in the world of culture and the arts and in many other areas of public life have united in expressing their revulsion at this monstrosity. Yet we are compelled to have the biggest stockpile of nuclear bombs in Europe landed on us, at Coulport on Loch Long. And it is from Faslane on the Gareloch that the boats sail out on their murderous and insane mission.

The official government policy is that it will negotiate Trident away when America and Russia have reduced their nuclear weapons to the level of Britain's – a meaningless and unprincipled posture that achieves nothing, and does nothing to move towards eliminating nuclear weapons. Likewise the government has opposed proposals at the United Nations to have a Treaty making a world-wide ban on nuclear weapons negotiated within a specific time scale. Indeed, far from Britain going nuclear-free, plans are already in hand for a replacement for Trident, a bigger and better version for the future. So much for working for a nuclear-free world, the government's election promise.

New Labour nuclear apologists raise their hands in collective sanctimonious horror when other countries – India and Pakistan – attempt to follow our lead. They seem to have no difficulty in recognising that nuclear weapons are illegal weapons of mass destruction when these are in the possession of a foreign state. Somehow, however, when these same weapons are in British hands, why then it's a different matter. Then they are magically transformed into something called a minimum deterrent (whatever that is), and are reclassified as the necessary and vital core of the UK's defence policy.

And what if other states should also consider that they too need this essential independent nuclear deterrent? What do we say to them? The hypocritical *"Don't do as I do, do as I say"* argument never convinced anyone.

New Labour's conversion to state sponsored nuclear terrorism is the most blatant and repulsive example of the leadership's willingness to abandon principal for reasons of perceived political expediency. In no other area of betrayal of humanitarian and socialistic principles, is the consequence so manifestly evil.

Trident is unique in its destructiveness. Apart from the unimaginable human carnage it promises, the use of even one of these submarines would produce a release of massive radioactive fallout which would cause devastating environmental damage. It is a naïve and perverse act of blind faith to delude ourselves that we could inflict such horrendous ecological damage on the planet, and yet believe that it – and we – could somehow subsequently carry on as normal. Trident is not, as many ignorant and foolish proponents seem to imagine, something like a bigger and better grenade.

To my mind there is no greater symbol of the gulf between genuine self-government, and the coming Scottish Parliament (welcome though it is), than the imposition of Trident on Scotland. The ability to decide the – literally – life and death question of war or peace is the acid test of a state's independence. The vital area of defence remains in Westminster hands.

In December 97 more than 60 generals and admirals from Britain, America, and all round the world signed a statement calling for the speedy abolition of all nuclear weapons. The statement was signed by Gen. Sir Hugo Beach, Field Marshal Lord Carver, Brigadier Harbottle and Air Commodore Alastair Mackie from Britain. Also by generals and admirals from Canada, Denmark, France, Ghana, Greece, India, Japan, Jordan, the Netherlands, Norway, Pakistan, Portugal, Russia and the United States.

One of the signatories was General Lee Butler, who is not just any retired general. For 33 years he was involved in every aspect of US nuclear weapons planning. He has been in the bomber cockpits, on submarines and in the missile silos. Under President Bush he personally selected thousands of targets in the former Soviet Union for mass destruction. He literally had his finger on the trigger. Now hear what he says: *"(deterrence) was based on a litany of false assumptions, unprovable assertions and logical contradictions. It suspended rational thinking about the ultimate aim of national security, to ensure the survival of the state....the Cold War lives on in the minds of those who cannot let go the fears, the beliefs, and the enmities born of the nuclear age. They cling to deterrence, clutch its tattered promise to their breast, shake it wistfully at bygone adversaries and balefully at new or imagined ones. They are gripped still by its awful willingness not simply to tempt the apocalypse, but to prepare its way"*.

Elsewhere he writes: *Nuclear war is a raging insatiable beast whose instincts and appetite we pretend to understand, but cannot possibly control... we have yet to grasp the monstrous effects of these weapons, that the consequences of their use defy reason, transcending time and space, poisoning the earth and deforming its inhabitants... The Cold War is over. We must not let it come back. We must achieve a world free of the threat of nuclear weapons, a nuclear free world. The price already*

187

paid is too dear, the risks too great. The task is daunting, but we cannot shrink from it. The opportunity may not come again."

Likewise in February 1998 more than 100 present and former heads of state and other civilian leaders also signed a statement expressing common concern regarding nuclear weapons, and endorsing a reasoned and speedy path towards abolition. The signatories included people of such international standing as Dennis Healy, James Callaghan, former US President Jimmy Carter, Mikhail Gorbachev, etc.

Thus we have the absurd situation that the Labour party, which supported nuclear abolition during the period of the Cold War, now supports the bomb when the alleged historical rationale – the so-called Soviet Threat – has disappeared, while on the other hand so many old cold warriors are now *en masse* abandoning the very doctrine of nuclear deterrence to which New Labour has become recent ardent converts.

New Labour has made this conversion – or should I say perversion – when we not only have generals and politicians expressing their disillusionment with the sacred doctrine of deterrence, but at a time when the whole force of international law is being mobilised against nuclear exterminism.

In July 1996 the International Court of Justice in the Hague ruled that the use or the threat of use of nuclear weapons generally violated international and humanitarian law. They affirmed that nuclear weapons were bound by the same rules of war that applied to any other type of weapon. The wilful killing of civilians remains a war crime whatever the technology involved.

It is important to realise that this judgement of the World Court was not an innovation. The Court does not make new laws – it interprets or explains ones already existing. These laws were previously codified in many international laws such as the Hague Conventions, the Geneva Conventions and the Nuremberg Principles. These statutes are in fact an affirmation of the basic Common Law principle that the lives of the innocent are always sacrosanct, in war as in peace.

The concept of a just war (*bellum iustum*) has always demanded not only that there be just cause to go to war in the first place (*ius **ad bellum***) – it has also always insisted that the war be conducted according to the principles of natural justice (*ius **in bello***). Thus, for example, rape, torture, the execution of prisoners of war or the deliberate killing of civilians have always been war crimes and are inexcusable, even if the commission if such acts is perceived to bring victory nearer. That is why the blanket bombing of Germany, like the atomic bombs on Hiroshima and Nagasaki were war crimes. To enrol in the honourable profession of arms is not to receive a licence to indulge in mere murder.

All of which brings us back full circle to the tents at Coulport and the Ploughshares 2000 movement; to our attempt to uphold the law, and stop the conspiracy to commit major war crimes that is implicit in nuclear deterrence.

I will close by repeating my conviction that it is the most solemn obligation on all of the people of Scotland to stand up against Trident and never to accept the imposition of the genocidal system on our land. Silence is consent.

August 31st 1998

Derick Thomson

Storming

"Land of mountains, glens and heroes:"
we have the glens and mountains still
and the farmers' productive plains
not to mention beaches and oysters,
laid-up fishing boats
and unfrequented moors,
Clyde retired,
islands sold to foreigners,
oil wells plundered
while we still talk about freedom.
Too many of our neighbours
are locked in thralldom:
yoked to tabloids and videos,
with drink and drugs
lifting them from despair
and returning them
to worse conditions.
We have made prisons for ourselves
and it is high time the heroes
returned
to storm this Bastille.

Ruaraidh MacThòmais

Creachadh

"Tìr nam beann, nan gleann 's nan gaisgeach:"
tha na glinn 's na beanntan againn fhathast
is còmhnardan tarbhach nan tuathanach,
gun luaidh air tràighean is eisirean,
eathraichean iasgaich air chiallaidh,
is mòintichean falamh de dhaoine,
Cluaidh air chluainidh,
eileanan gan reic ri eilthirich
is tobraichean ola gan spùinneadh,
is sinn fhathast a' bruidhinn mu shaorsa.
Ach tha cus de ar coimhearsnaich
glaiste ann an daorsa:
fo chuing nan tabloid 's nam video,
deoch is drogaichean
gan togail à dorainn
's gan tilleadh
gu staid nas miosa.
Rinn sinn prìosanan dhuinn fhìn
's tha thìd aig na gaisgich
tilleadh
's am Bastille seo a chreachadh.

The Iceberg

When the iceberg moves
from the ancient shore,
when the split widens
and the crack comes,
it will move north
slowly,
whether or not we get divisions
between tenant and landlord
or Queen.
I hope
that our hopes are not vain
and that there is earth under the ice
from which plants will burgeon
and life come,
and that we won't have to wait as long
as some think
until the trees grow
and the people develop
to steer the land
to a new harbour
where ice does not weigh down our expectation.

A' Bheinn-Eighre

Nuair a ghluaiseas a' bheinn-eighre
bhon t-seann chladach,
nuair a leudaicheas an sgàineadh,
's a thig am brag,
gluaisidh i gu tuath
air a socair,
as bith an tig sgaradh
eadar tuath is tighearna
no Bàn-righ.
Tha mi 'n dòchas
nach bi ar dòchas faoin
's gu bheil fonn fon deigh
ás am brùchd lusan
's ás an gluais beatha,
's nach bi againn ri fuireach cho fada
's a tha cuid am barail
gus a fàs na craobhan
's gus an cinnich na daoine
a stiùireas i
gu acarsaid ùr
anns nach laigh deigh air dùil.

J. N. Reilly

A Wee Turkey and A Sprig Of Mistletoe

Dark already, he muttered absently for the umpteenth time, passing the kitchen, buttoning his coat. He stuck his head into the living-room.

See you later girls, he called out to his daughters.

See you Daddy, they called back, too involved with watching television to look round, at ease in the safety and comfort of home.

Sue and Sally, being seven and nine years old, had Santa on their minds, cosy in yuletide reveries. Stephanie, sprawled out in front of the electric fire was eleven, knew there was no Santa, but didn't tell. She loved Christmas although she was growing up now, and you don't get so many toys. She felt a little pang of guilt at even thinking of toys; an involuntary admission to herself that she wasn't quite as grown up as she liked to think herself. But she didn't care, she was happy being eleven.

Now, a two pint carton of milk. That's all I want you to get, said his wife, coming from the kitchen. Then, playfully: And I want to see change from that pound.

He leaned over and kissed her nose.

I don't know if I'll be able to manage that, he rejoined.

She squeezed his arm.

You won't get much of a walk if you don't go now, she said, adding: It's freezing cold out there. The pavements are icy, so watch yourself.

Okay. I will. See you later.

Bye.

He pulled up the collar of his coat as he stepped out of the close. Turning left, he hurried up the street, the air sharp at his throat. His wife hadn't exaggerated. It was freezing cold. Too cold for a leisurely walk, he decided, he would just go to the newsagent's at the shopping mall, buy the milk and get home to a good warm fire. The sensible thing to do. But it was such a lovely early evening, clear and glistening, the first stars appearing above the tenements, the perfect setting to lose himself in, to merge with, to escape the knowledge of his poverty, the bemused sense of no future which now and then insidiously pervaded him until he had no sense of anything but despair.

The tenement windows glowed brightly, sprinkled with christmas trees and fairy lights. Through some of the windows of the ground floor flats he could see colourful tissue and tinsel decorations hanging from ceilings and cards pinned to walls. A cheering sight, with more children sitting expectantly around televisions.

At the top of the street he crossed Farmers Road and made his way across the wasteground where trees had once stood. In the distance , a bonfire blazed. He made his way towards it. Usually when it was dark he avoided crossing the wasteground and took the long way round it. Too many folk had been attacked and robbed. However, it being such a clear evening, and with the bonfire blazing, he would be able to see anyone approaching, and if necessary was prepared to run.

The earth was frozen solid under his feet, the untrodden grass glistening with frost, as if reflecting the starlight. He sighed wistfully when gazing at the frost, and the stars in the great crystal dome of sky around him, somehow beckoning , and the more he gazed, the more he saw, the more he didn't want to look, until he didn't want to see. Winter's glory now reminded him of all he had lost, of all he didn't have, of his poverty, of the poverty in this forgotten corner of the city; and that concealed by the warm lights from too many of the tenement windows were cold bones and hearts and hopes, chillier than any winter could ever be. He bowed his head and hurried on, angry with himself.

Some boys and young men stood around the bonfire heating and rubbing their hands. He kept his eyes on them lest one should strike out, even if he was only fifty metres or so away from Roselaw Street with its lamplight and activity, it being the street leading to the shopping mall.

He welcomed the heat of the fire brushing his face as he passed it.

Have you got a spare cigarette on you, mate? A young man barely in his twenties ominously called out to him.

I don't smoke, sorry, he replied and quickened his pace, glad to leave them behind and turn onto the street. A couple of boys were playing football on the pavement, laughing as they slid and fell on the ice. He followed the street. At first there were tenements to his left and trees to his right, then a block of tenements on either side of him, then the shopping mall at the end of the street, encircled by more trees.

He blinked and adjusted his focus in the glare from the mall's enormous illuminated sign above the entrance. Desperate for warmth, he hurried past the queue at the bus stop and shoppers with bulging polythene bags into the dazzling mall. Its heat loosened the tension which had begun to oppress him and relaxed him a little. He went straight to the newsagent's and purchased the milk. He didn't bother himself with looking at the window displays. There would be no point in it.

Not wanting to test his luck by crossing the wasteground twice in one evening, he left the mall by a side exit to cross the car park and take the path through the trees, which would soon take him onto Roselaw Street and the long way round the wasteground.

The bitter cold air took his breath away. He was just about to make his way between two delivery trucks when he saw the back door of one lying open, revealing open-topped boxes of turkeys and chickens. There was no one around, no sight or sound of driver or anyone.

Should I? he said inwardly, his heart now thumping at the thought.

Bugger it, he muttered, took a fowl and headed quickly for the path. He had just reached it when:

Hey, you. You thieving swine.

There had been someone sitting quietly in the cab of the truck.

Just my bloody luck, he said to himself and ran, amazing himself with the speed of his sprint. Intuitively he ran into the darkness of the woods, in fear of being identified. Knowing it would be stupid to run in the direction of Roselaw Street, he ran to his left, behind the mall, dodging between the trees, barely keeping his footing, thankful for the clear evening or he wouldn't have been able to run between the trees with such agility, the bird under one arm, the milk under the other.

Just my bloody luck. Stupid bloody fool. Stupid...

The cold air was hurting his throat. He was losing strength. He couldn't run anymore.

Surely no one would follow me into here. Not for a wee turkey.

Slowed to walking pace, he stopped and listened. Not a sound of pursuit, just distant traffic. He could still see lights from the mall.

Don't be stupid. No one's following, he said to himself and sighed with relief.

The ground gradually rose to a steep ascent which led him up out of the silvery dimness of the woods onto the bank of the canal and into the soft brilliance of a big round moon. He felt more at ease now he was out of the woods and could look around himself, feeling safe, in the wintry crisp silence. Momentarily taken by how close and big the moon seemed, he lost no time in hurrying along the dirt path by the canal bank, leaving the mall behind him somewhere to his left, beyond the trees, thanking his good fortune, and laughing and shaking his head at his folly. It didn't take him long to reach Farmers Lock, which had long since decayed, and the old stone steps to the path by the canal on its lower level. But his mounting satisfaction was shattered when:

Stop, you bastard...

He couldn't believe it. He looked back quickly. Someone was at the top of the steps. He couldn't believe he had been followed or somehow caught in possession of the turkey. Then he saw a large knife in the man's hand, glinting in the moonlight. He ran, still firmly holding onto the turkey and milk, the sound of the man with the knife chasing after him, repeatedly shouting: Stop, you heathen bastard, stop...

Oh no...

It didn't feel as if he had an option. His previous escape had sapped his strength. His legs were getting weaker and weaker, his breathing too painful. He couldn't go on. He stumbled to his knees, his back ending up against the trunk of a tree, the turkey and milk still under his arms.

Got you, you heathen...

The man raised the knife...

Oh it's yourself, said the man.

He stared at him, shocked silent in disbelief and bewilderment, to dazed to feel afraid. He didn't know the greasy unshaven face grinning into his astonishment.

Don't you know me? Don't you remember me? Have you not seen me about the place, said the man. I live across the backcourt from you.

He opened his mouth. Only the steam from his breath rose into the air, and then:

Is that so.

That's right, said the man, you remember me now, eh. I'm sorry I gave you a wee fright, but I was after that bastard of a pal of mine. You don't thieve from a pal, do you? I was waiting up there at the lock to ambush him. I'll get back. I don't want to miss him. See you around. Watch yourself.

What a life. It couldn't be real. He watched the man disappear into the darkness, swinging the knife nonchalantly by his side. He didn't make a

197

move to rise. He turned his gaze to the moon, enormous above the treetops, brilliantly white yet soft to the eyes, he saw it as fondant, forever melting, and felt a yielding beauty, charming and soothing him.

Rested and relaxed, he was just about to rise when he noticed something on his shoulder. A sprig of mistletoe. He smiled, put the milk on the ground, put the mistletoe in his coat pocket and got to his feet. He thought the mistletoe must have fallen from a tree. The milk and turkey once again secure under his arms, he made for home. He didn't have too far to go.

Is that you? his wife called out as soon as he opened the door.

Yes, he called back. Just me.

I thought the cold would have brought you back sooner.

I went for a walk after all, he said, entering the living-room.

His wife was sitting in the chair by the fire, Stephanie at her feet. He kissed her and: I'll put these into the fridge and take my coat off. I got a wee turkey for fifty pence, he said, not knowing what to say about how the turkey came into his possession, holding it up and adding: It probably fell off the back of a lorry.

That's not a turkey, said his wife, pointing at the writing on its wrapper. Look, it's a duck.

He laughed, she laughed, and the girls, who had begun singing along with the carol singing on television, told them to be quiet.

Laughing to himself he put the milk and duck in the fridge and went to his bedroom and took off his coat and shoes. He hadn't forgotten the mistletoe and took it from his pocket. As he looked at it he was determined to do all he could to secure a better life for his family, even if that meant staring something new, learning something new, no matter how long it might take.

The sweet voices of his wife and daughters, joined with the choir on television, drifted through to him.

Silent night, holy night…

God, he sighed, I never remember the words to that song.

He listened. There was a painful beauty in their voices. The room cool around him. The moon at the window.

All is calm, all is right…

Sweet Jesus, just a bit of luck, he said, just a bit of luck.

He put the mistletoe on the dressing-table and closed the curtains on the moon.

Contributors

Donald Anderson: Taught Modern Studies and History in Glasgow Secondary Schools. Active in Scottish Republican Movement.

Freddy Anderson: Born in Ballybay, Co. Monachan, Eire in 1922 in the first year of the Irish Republic. Educated in National School, then Roscrea College, Co. Tipperary, and University College, Dublin. Volunteered for the R.A.F; Britain and Burma in the anti-fascist war (1942-45). Was one of the four poets in the Glasgow collection *Fowrsom Reel (1947)* – prefaced by Hugh MacDairmid. His short stories have been broadcast by BBC Scotland and Radio Eireanne. He won the Scotsman Award (1979) for his John MacLean play *Krassivy* and also The Irish Post Award (1989) for his satiric Irish novel and play *Oiny Hoy*. Currently involved in a book entitled *Glasgow Burnsiana,* a collection of Irish short stories and a continuation of Oiny Hoy's incredible adventures in a crazy world.

John Taylor Caldwell: Worked with the United Socialist Movement founded by Guy Aldred and worked on the Strickland Press for thirty years, taking over the editorship of The Word on Aldred's death. He has collected and collated *The Writings of Guy Aldred* and written a biography of Aldred, *Come Dungeons Dark (Luath Press).* He is also the author of an autobiography, *Severely Dealt With (Northern Herald Books, 1993).*

Myles Campbell: Known in Gaelic as Maoilios Caimbeul. Collections of his poetry include *Eileann (Celtic Dept. Glasgow University, 1980), Bailtean (Gairm, Glasgow, 1987), A' Caradh an Rathaid (Coisceim, Dublin, 1988)* and *A' Gabhail Ris (Gairm, 1994). Bailtean* is bilingual, the other collections are in Gaelic.

Alex Cathcart: His short stories and poems have been published in various magazines and anthologies. He is the author of two novels, *The Comeback (Polygon, 1985)* and *The Missionary (Polygon, 1987).* He has a novel ready for publication and is working on another.

Joanna Clarke: BSc. MIBiol. AIBMS. CBiol. The Scottish Consumers Association for Natural Food.

Sean Clerkin: Organiser of the National Petition Against Poverty.

Louise Cockburn: Assistant to the National Convenor of the Scottish National Party, Alex Salmond MP.

Vernon Coleman: The author of over 85 international best-selling books including *Mindpower, Toxic Stress* and over a dozen novels. He worked as a family and hospital doctor for ten years before retiring to write full time. He lives in a secluded country home in the depths of the English countryside. He is the Health Spokesman for the newly formed Democratic Party.

David Craig: Collections of poetry include *Latest News (1978), Homing (1981), Against Looting (1986), The Grasshopper's Burden (ARC, 1991).* He has written three novels, *The Rebels* and *The Hostage(with Nigel Gray, 1978), King Cameron(Carcanet,* 1992) and has newly completed *The Unbroken Harp.* Other works; *Native Stones(Secker, 1987), On The Crofter's Trail(Cape, 1990)* and *Landmarks(Cape, 1995).* All are available in Pimlico pb. He is working on a series for TV based on Landmarks.

Prof. Richard Demarco: OBE, Fellow of the Royal Society of Art, Hon. Fellow of the Royal Incorporation of Architects of Scotland, Chevalier des Lettres de Francais, Cavalieri de la Republica d'Ialia, Gold Order of Merit of the Peoples' Republic of Poland, first recipient of the Arts Medal of the Royal Philosophical Society, Glasgow. He is the art advisor to the Euoropean Youth Parliament. He has lectured in hundreds of universities and art schools in North America, Australasia and Europe and presented well over 1000 exhibitions and productions in theatre and art. Publications include *The Road to Meikle Seggie, The Artist as Explorer* and *A Life in Pictures.*

Hugh Dodd: A cartoonist, artist and author, he has contributed to many national newspapers and journals. Recent publications include *A Good Wigging, Tales from the Turf* and *Barrels of Fun.*

Graham Fulton: Former member of Itinerant Poets performance group. His work has appeared in numerous magazines and anthologies and has been broadcast on radio and television. Collections include *The Eighth Dwarf (Itinerant Publications)* and *Humouring the Iron Bar Man* and *Knights of the Lower Floor,* both published by Polygon.

William Hershaw: Principal Teacher of English at Beath High School, Cowdenbeath. He plays guitar and mandolin in the folk group *Touch The Earth.* The Scottish Cultural Press published his *The Cowdenbeath Man,* poems in Scots and English in 1997.

John Manson: Retired crofter and teacher. An active translator and critic he was awarded his first SAC bursary for translation three years ago. Contributed to numerous anthologies and magazines such as Cencrastus, Chapman and Lines Review. Publications; *Hugh MacDairmid, Selected Poems (Penguin 1970), East Sutherland and Other Poems(Reidhmasach Press 1985), Malevich in Edinburgh(Markings Publications 1997).* His translation of *White Sea* by *Victor Serge* is forthcoming from the Penniless Press.

Farquhar McLay: Wrote mainly for the BBC during the late '50s and throughout the '60s. Published in various magazines including The Listener, Edinburgh Review, Chapman. Edited *Voices of Dissent, Workers City* and *The Reckoning,* all published by the Clydeside Press. He is currently finishing a novel.

Gordon Meade: Educated at the Universities of Dundee and Newcastle Upon Tyne. Has been awarded three SAC Writers' Bursaries and participated in two British Council reading tours of Germany and Belgium. From 1993 to 1995 he was the Fellow in Creative Writing at the Duncan of Jordanstone College of Art and Writer in Residence for Dundee District Libraries. He has two collections of poetry, *Singing Seals(1991)* and *The Scrimshaw Sailor(1996)* published by Chapman, Edinburgh.

William Neill: Widely published in magazines and anthologies. Collections include *Sruth na Maoile* and *Selected Poems 1969-1992(Canongate)* and *Galloway Landscapes (Previous Parrot Press).*

Sarah North: Works for Greenpeace UK, Canonbury Villas, London.

Brian Quail: Peace activist and member of Ploughshare 2000. Joint Secretary of the Scottish Campaign for Nuclear Disarmament. To all who share the commitment to stop Trident, Brian sends a warm invitation to join in Ploughshare 2000. Please contact him on 0141-339-1482 for further details or more information about Scottish CND.

J. N. Reilly: Raised and schooled in Easterhouse where he discovered and got involved with composition and painting and wrote his first poems and prose. Since moving west his stories, poems, translations and extracts from his prose works have been widely published. If you wonder why some of the older generation of Scottish writers and some of their younger contemporaries no longer use speech marks then blame J. N. Reilly who disposed of them in the '70s and had to fight in the late '80s to keep them out of his work. In one instance he complained to the then editors of NWS that the managing editor had refused to publish his work without speech marks, his work was reinstated, but he was never again published in NWS. One wonders what those writers reply on their reading and lecture tours when asked why they no longer use speech marks. Works for future publication include his translation of *The Complete Works of Arthur Rimbaud, A Knife on a Country Road, The Doleful and 3 Beautiful stories.* He scatters big medicine, the word... You know what the word is, don't you?

Dee Rimbaud: it is not just about aspiring to the sublime, but something to do with the twisted pleasure of pain/catharsis is about burning/better to burn than drown in mediocrity/this sentiment is not just my own/it is a universal archetype which speaks to the viscera, spirit and soul/everyone understands this deep inside/most folk try to ignore it/prefer an ignoble life saturated in platitudes/those of us who nurture the wee embers burning inside desire the apocalyptic/that's why we write/we want to spread the fire...

Bill Robertson: From a mining family, brought up in the pit rows of Fife. He was chief reporter and then features editor of the Daily Record in the 1960s and '70s. Later he was one of the editorial team that launched the Sunday Standard. For the past 15 years he has freelanced, covering Glasgow City Council on a daily basis for the national press and TV.

Fr. Willy Slavin: RC Chaplain in HMP Barlinnie 1982-1992 and formerly co-ordinator of the Scottish Drugs Forum. He is an educational psychologist and currently consultant to a programme for juvenile drug users in Notre Dame Family Centre's adolescent unit in Downhill, Glasgow.

Derick Thomson: Writes in Gaelic as Ruaraidh MacThómais and has published widely in Gaelic and English, including *An Introduction to Gaelic Poetry, The Companion to Gaelic Scotland* and seven collections of poetry. His *Collected Poems, Creachadh na Clàrsaich / Plundering the Harp,* and his latest collection *Meall Garbh / The Ragged Mountain,* are both available from Gairm Publications, Glasgow.

Jeff Torrington: Published in various magazines and anthologies. His novel *Swing Hammer Swing* won the Whitbread Prize, followed by *The Devils Carousel,* both published by Secker and Warburg. Currently working on two novels including *Go Down Laughing.*

Richie Venton: Scottish Socialist Party trade union organiser and West of Scotland organiser.

Les Ward: Author of and contributor to a number of reports and articles on various animal welfare/protection matters. He is the Director of Advocates for Animals, Assistant Secretary, St. Andrew Animal Fund, Member of the Home Secretary's Animal Procedures Committee, Founder of The Boyd Group on animal experiments, Trustee of Lord Houghton Memorial Fund, Marchig Animal Welfare Trust and Patron of Felix Cat Rescue.

Bill Williams: Printer and publisher based in the North East of Scotland. His arts free sheet, *ArtWork*, prides itself on eschewing any form of public or private patronage. Earlier ventures have included the weekly radical Glasgow News and the original community newspaper The Gorbals View. He was principal agitator in the STORM campaign to fight the madness of rail privatisation and is planning a millennium protest against the dominance of Lottery funding in the arts and so much more of our public life.

James D. Young: Socialist historian, writer and speaker. Contributor to various magazines, anthologies and newspapers including The Herald, Irish Post and Times Educational Supplement. Was Reader in History at Stirling University. Publications include *The Rousing of the Scottish Working Class (Croom Helm, 1979), Women and Popular Struggles (Mainstream, 1985), Making Trouble (Clydeside Press, 1987).* Forthcoming books include *The World of C.L.R. James: The Unfragmented Vision.*